# Living with Victim Mentality

## Shifting the Mindset from Victim to Victor

By Courtney Collins

Living with Victim Mentality

# Table of Contents

Living with Victim Mentality

# Chapter 1:

# Understanding Victim Mentality

Victim mentality is a pervasive mindset where individuals perceive themselves as powerless, consistently believing that they are at the mercy of external circumstances, other people, or their past experiences. This mentality often traps individuals in a cycle of blame, self-pity, and helplessness, preventing them from taking proactive steps to improve their situation. To fully understand victim mentality, it's essential to delve into its roots, psychological underpinnings, and how it manifests in various aspects of life.

**Defining Victim Mentality**

Victim mentality is not just about feeling sad or having a bad day; it is a deeply ingrained belief system that repeatedly casts oneself as the victim in most situations. People with this mindset often feel that life is happening "to them" rather than being something they can actively shape. They may frequently feel wronged, mistreated, or unlucky and tend to blame their circumstances, other people, or past events for their problems. This mindset can become a default way of thinking, trapping individuals in a cycle of negative emotions and self-defeating behaviour.

Some key characteristics of victim mentality include:

1. **Blame**: The tendency to blame others or external circumstances for personal failures or misfortunes.

2. **Helplessness**: A pervasive sense of powerlessness, feeling incapable of changing or improving one's situation.

3. **Negative Thinking**: Persistent pessimism and focus on the worst possible outcomes.

4. **Self-Pity**: An excessive focus on one's misfortunes, often accompanied by a desire for sympathy or validation from others.

5. **Avoidance of Responsibility**: An unwillingness to take accountability for one's actions, often deflecting responsibility onto others or external factors.

**Roots of Victim Mentality: Past Experiences, Trauma, and Learned Behaviour**

Victim mentality doesn't develop overnight; it usually has deep-seated roots that can be traced back to past experiences, trauma, or learned behaviour from family, culture, or society. Understanding these origins is crucial for recognizing why this mindset develops and how it becomes ingrained.

1. **Past Experiences and Trauma**:

   Traumatic experiences, especially those occurring during childhood, can significantly contribute to the development of a victim mentality. Trauma can include abuse, neglect, bullying, or significant loss. When someone goes through these painful events, they often feel powerless, and these feelings can linger long after the trauma has passed. The brain, in an attempt to protect itself, may adopt a victim mentality as a defence mechanism. By perceiving oneself as a perpetual victim, the mind tries to justify feelings of pain, sadness, and anger, creating a narrative that these feelings are not only valid but unavoidable.

For example, a person who experienced emotional neglect as a child might grow up feeling unworthy of love or care, constantly seeking validation but never believing they truly deserve it. This can lead to a pattern of blaming others when things go wrong, as it reinforces the belief that they are inherently unlucky or doomed to suffer.

2. **Learned Behaviour**:

Victim mentality can also be a learned behaviour, often modelled by parents, caregivers, or significant others. Children absorb and mimic the attitudes and behaviours they observe, so if a child grows up in an environment where a parent frequently complains, blames others, or refuses to take responsibility, the child may adopt similar patterns. This learned victimhood becomes a familiar, albeit unhealthy, way of coping with challenges.

Additionally, cultural and societal influences can reinforce this mindset. For instance, if a community normalizes a "blame culture," where people routinely deflect accountability and criticize others for their own problems, it can foster an environment where victim mentality thrives.

3. **Psychological and Emotional Aspects**:

Victim mentality is deeply tied to psychological and emotional factors. Individuals with this mindset often suffer from low self-esteem, anxiety, and depression. The persistent negative self-talk and inner dialogue reinforce the belief that they are incapable of overcoming their challenges. Emotionally, there is often a deep-seated fear of failure, rejection, or abandonment, which fuels the need to blame others or external factors rather than facing the discomfort of personal responsibility.

Cognitive distortions, such as catastrophizing (expecting the worst to happen) or personalization (assuming everything is directed at oneself), further exacerbate victim mentality. These thought patterns create a distorted view of reality where the individual sees themselves as powerless and always at the receiving end of bad luck or mistreatment.

## Manifestations of Victim Mentality in Daily Life, Work, and Relationships

Victim mentality doesn't remain confined to thoughts; it infiltrates every aspect of life, including daily routines, professional settings, and personal relationships. Recognizing how this mindset manifests can help individuals identify the impact it has on their overall quality of life.

1. **Daily Life:**

   In daily life, victim mentality can manifest as chronic complaining, procrastination, and a lack of motivation. Individuals with this mindset often feel overwhelmed by even minor setbacks and may constantly seek validation or sympathy from others. Simple tasks become burdensome because the individual believes that nothing ever goes right for them.

For example, a person with a victim mentality might repeatedly complain about their commute, blaming traffic, the weather, or other drivers for their tardiness rather than considering ways to adjust their schedule or find alternative routes. This behaviour reinforces the belief that they have no control over their circumstances.

2. **Work Life**

   In professional settings, victim mentality can severely hinder career growth and job satisfaction. Employees who perceive themselves as victims often struggle with taking initiative, accepting feedback, or engaging in constructive problem-solving. They may frequently blame colleagues, management, or company policies for their lack of progress, rather than taking proactive steps to improve their performance or skill set.

For instance, an employee who consistently feels overlooked for promotions may blame office politics or favouritism without reflecting on their own work habits, attitude, or willingness to take on new responsibilities. This mindset not only stalls their career but also creates a toxic work environment, as it can breed resentment and a lack of teamwork.

3. **Relationships**:

In personal relationships, victim mentality can be especially damaging. It often leads to patterns of passive-aggressive communication, constant complaining, and an inability to empathize with others. The person with a victim mentality may feel perpetually misunderstood, mistreated, or unappreciated, leading to conflicts and emotional distance.

For example, in a romantic relationship, one partner may constantly accuse the other of not caring enough, always focusing on perceived slights or unfulfilled expectations. This can create a cycle of blame and defensiveness, eroding trust and intimacy. Over time, the relationship may become strained or even break down due to the relentless negativity and lack of accountability.

## Why Victim Mentality Persists

Victim mentality persists because it provides a sense of comfort, even though it is ultimately self-destructive. The narrative of being a victim can feel safer than the uncertainty of taking responsibility, facing fears, or making changes. It allows individuals to avoid difficult emotions like guilt, shame, or fear of failure, by placing the blame elsewhere. This avoidance, however, comes at a high cost: it keeps individuals trapped in a cycle of negativity, preventing them from reaching their full potential.

1. **Secondary Gains**:

Sometimes, victim mentality is reinforced by the secondary gains it provides. This might include receiving attention, sympathy, or validation from others, which can be temporarily gratifying. These external affirmations can create a feedback loop that keeps the victim mindset in place because, subconsciously, the individual feels rewarded for their complaints and perceived helplessness.

2. **Fear of Responsibility and Change**:

Taking responsibility for one's actions and mindset requires facing uncomfortable truths and making changes, which can be daunting. It's often easier to remain in a familiar, albeit unhappy, state of victimhood than to confront the fear of change, failure, or rejection. This avoidance of responsibility perpetuates the cycle of blame and helplessness.

3. **Lack of Skills or Awareness**:

Many people with a victim mentality are unaware of their thought patterns or do not have the skills needed to break free from them. Without self-awareness or the tools to manage negative thoughts, the victim mindset can feel like an insurmountable part of their identity.

## Conclusion

Understanding victim mentality is the first step toward breaking free from its grip. It is a complex interplay of past experiences, learned behaviours, and deep-seated emotional and psychological patterns that shape how individuals perceive themselves and their place in the world. Recognizing the signs of victim mentality in daily life, work, and relationships can empower individuals to take the next steps toward change. By acknowledging the roots of this mindset and the impact it has on overall well-being, one can begin the journey from feeling powerless to reclaiming control and living a more empowered and fulfilling life.

# Chapter 2:

# The Power of Negative Thoughts

Negative thoughts are powerful forces that shape our perceptions, influence our decisions, and ultimately dictate the quality of our lives. They are the mental seeds from which victim mentality often grows, feeding a cycle of self-doubt, helplessness, and perpetual dissatisfaction. Understanding negative thinking patterns and how they intertwine with victim mentality is crucial for breaking free from these destructive mental habits. This chapter will explore the nature of negative thoughts, delve into common negative thinking patterns, and examine how these thoughts shape our perceptions and decisions.

## Defining Negative Thinking Patterns and Their Connection to Victim Mentality

Negative thinking patterns are habitual ways of interpreting and responding to events in a pessimistic, self-defeating manner. They are automatic, deeply ingrained thought processes that skew reality, focusing on the worst aspects of any situation while disregarding positive or neutral elements. These patterns often lead to feelings of anxiety, depression, and hopelessness, creating a distorted mental landscape where problems feel insurmountable, and opportunities seem non-existent.

Negative thinking is closely linked to victim mentality because it reinforces the belief that one is powerless and at the mercy of circumstances. When someone consistently interprets events through a negative lens, they are more likely to feel wronged, mistreated, or unlucky. This mental state feeds the victim mindset, creating a vicious cycle where negative thoughts perpetuate feelings of helplessness and self pity, further entrenching the belief that life is inherently unfair.

The impact of negative thinking on daily life can be profound. It affects self-esteem, motivation, and relationships, leading individuals to make choices that reinforce their negative worldview. Instead of seeing challenges as opportunities for growth, negative thinkers see them as proof that they are doomed to fail. This mindset can hinder personal and professional development, as the individual becomes trapped in a self-fulfilling prophecy of negativity and victimhood.

**Types of Negative Thoughts**

Negative thoughts can take many forms, each with its own unique way of distorting reality and reinforcing a victim mindset. Some of the most common types of negative thinking include catastrophizing, black-and-white thinking, and self-blame. These patterns are not just fleeting thoughts; they are habitual ways of interpreting the world that significantly impact decision-making and overall quality of life.

1. **Catastrophizing**

   Catastrophizing is a thinking pattern where individuals consistently expect the worst possible outcome in any situation. This form of negative thinking amplifies problems, blowing them out of proportion and turning minor setbacks into major crises. People who catastrophize often jump to the worst-case scenario without considering more likely, less dramatic possibilities.

For example, if someone receives critical feedback at work, rather than viewing it as a chance to improve, they might immediately think, "I'm going to lose my job," or "I'm a complete failure." This mindset causes excessive anxiety and fear, making it difficult to respond rationally to challenges. Catastrophizing is a core component of victim mentality because it reinforces the belief that the world is an unpredictable and dangerous place where disaster is always looming.

Catastrophizing affects decision-making by leading individuals to avoid taking risks or trying new things due to an overwhelming fear of failure. It creates a paralyzing sense of dread, preventing personal growth and fostering a persistent sense of vulnerability. By always expecting the worst, catastrophizers live in a state of constant alert, draining their mental and emotional resources and perpetuating a cycle of helplessness and inaction.

2. **Black-and-White Thinking**

Black-and-white thinking, also known as all-or-nothing thinking, is a cognitive distortion where individuals view situations in extremes, without recognizing the nuances or middle ground. In this mindset, things are either completely good or entirely bad, with no room for grey areas. This type of thinking is rigid and unforgiving, leading to unrealistic expectations of oneself and others.

For instance, someone with black-and-white thinking might believe, "If I don't get this job, I'm a total failure," or "If my partner doesn't agree with me, they don't care about me at all." This pattern of thought creates a world where minor imperfections or disagreements are perceived as major flaws, leading to intense emotional reactions and a sense of perpetual disappointment.

Black-and-white thinking fuels victim mentality by creating a mental environment where anything less than perfect is unacceptable and feels like a personal attack. This rigid thinking style prevents individuals from seeing alternative perspectives or solutions, trapping them in a cycle of blame and resentment. When things don't go as planned, the person feels wronged or mistreated, reinforcing the belief that they are a victim of circumstances beyond their control.

This type of thinking also leads to poor decision-making. Because there is no room for compromise or flexibility, black-

and-white thinkers often make impulsive or extreme choices, such as quitting a job after one bad day or ending a relationship over a single disagreement. These decisions are driven by the belief that if something isn't perfect, it must be entirely wrong, leaving little room for growth, improvement, or understanding.

3.  **Self-Blame**

    Self-blame is a thinking pattern where individuals internalize negative events as being entirely their fault, even when they have little to no control over the situation. This mindset can be particularly damaging because it not only lowers self-esteem but also fosters feelings of guilt, shame, and unworthiness. People who engage in self-blame often believe that they are fundamentally flawed or inadequate, which reinforces their victim mentality by making them feel perpetually at fault.

For example, after a failed project, a person who engages in self-blame might think, "This happened because I'm incompetent," rather than considering external factors that contributed to the outcome. This thought process ignores the complexity of most situations, placing undue responsibility on oneself while failing to acknowledge external influences or shared accountability.

Self-blame is deeply connected to victim mentality because it keeps individuals stuck in a loop of self-punishment and regret. Instead of learning from mistakes and moving forward, self-blamers dwell on their perceived failures, reinforcing a narrative of personal inadequacy and helplessness. This cycle not only impacts mental health but also affects how they interact with others, often leading to withdrawal, avoidance, and a reluctance to take on new challenges for fear of repeated failure.

In decision-making, self-blame can lead to paralysis, where the individual is so consumed by fear of making the "wrong" choice that they avoid making decisions altogether. Alternatively, they may make overly cautious decisions that limit their growth, driven by the belief that they are inherently prone to failure. This perpetuates a stagnant, self-defeating cycle where the person remains trapped in their negative beliefs.

## How Negative Thoughts Shape Perceptions and Decisions

Negative thoughts act as a lens through which individuals view the world, shaping their perceptions and influencing their decisions in profound ways. When these thoughts dominate, they create a distorted version of reality that is coloured by fear, doubt, and pessimism. This distorted perception can have far-reaching effects on every aspect of life, from personal goals to relationships and career choices.

1. **Skewed Perception of Reality**

    Negative thoughts warp reality, making problems seem bigger and more insurmountable than they truly are. For instance, a person who constantly thinks they are unlucky will start to notice only the bad things that happen to them, ignoring any positive experiences. This selective attention reinforces their negative beliefs, creating a feedback loop that strengthens their victim mentality.

Over time, this skewed perception becomes a self-fulfilling prophecy. When you expect failure, rejection, or disappointment, you unconsciously make choices that align with these expectations. For example, someone who believes they are destined to be unhappy in relationships might repeatedly choose partners who are emotionally unavailable, reinforcing their belief that they are unworthy of love.

2. **Impact on Decision-Making**

    Negative thinking significantly impairs decision-making by fostering fear-based choices. Instead of evaluating options objectively, individuals dominated by negative thoughts often choose the path of least resistance or avoid making decisions altogether. This can lead to a pattern of indecision, missed opportunities, and settling for less than what one is capable of achieving.

For instance, a person with a negative mindset might stay in a job they dislike because they fear failure if they try something new. This reluctance to take risks stems from the belief that any change will inevitably lead to a worse outcome. As a result, they remain stuck in unsatisfying situations, reinforcing their belief that they are powerless to improve their circumstances.

3. **Self-Fulfilling Prophecies**

Negative thoughts often lead to self-fulfilling prophecies, where individuals unintentionally create the very outcomes they fear. If someone constantly tells themselves, "I'm not good enough," they may unconsciously behave in ways that confirm this belief, such as procrastinating, avoiding challenges, or failing to put in effort. When the predicted failure occurs, it reinforces the initial negative belief, further entrenching the victim mentality.

These self-fulfilling prophecies not only affect personal success but also impact how others perceive and interact with the individual. A person who consistently acts from a place of fear or negativity may be seen as lacking confidence or drive, leading to fewer opportunities and reinforcing their belief that they are inherently disadvantaged.

4. **Impact on Relationships**

Negative thinking can poison relationships by creating misunderstandings, conflict, and emotional distance. When someone interprets interactions through a negative lens, they are more likely to assume ill intent, feel unappreciated, or become defensive. For example, if a friend cancels plans, a person with a negative mindset might think, "They don't really care about me," rather than considering more benign explanations like a busy schedule.

These distorted perceptions lead to poor communication and a lack of trust, as negative thinkers often project their insecurities onto others. This behaviour can drive a wedge between people, as constant negativity becomes draining and difficult to manage in any relationship. Over time, these repeated patterns can lead to isolation, reinforcing the belief that the individual is destined to be alone or misunderstood.

## Conclusion

Negative thoughts are powerful forces that shape our realities, influencing how we perceive ourselves, others, and the world around us. By understanding the different types of negative thinking—such as catastrophizing, black-and-white thinking, and self-blame—we can begin to see how these patterns feed into victim mentality and perpetuate a cycle of helplessness and dissatisfaction.

These negative thoughts not only skew our perception of reality but also influence our decisions, often leading us down paths that confirm our deepest fears and insecurities. Recognizing and challenging these thought patterns is the first step toward breaking free from their hold, allowing us to reclaim control over our minds, our decisions, and ultimately, our lives. By learning to reframe negative thoughts, we can begin to dismantle the victim mentality and create a more empowered, fulfilling future.

# Chapter 3:

# Recognizing the Symptoms of Victim Mentality in Daily Life

Recognizing the symptoms of victim mentality is a crucial step in understanding how this mindset affects various aspects of daily life. Victim mentality manifests in many subtle and overt ways, often becoming so ingrained that individuals may not even realize they are trapped in a self-defeating cycle. By identifying these symptoms, individuals can start to challenge their negative beliefs and take steps toward change. In this chapter, we will explore the key symptoms of victim mentality, including self-pity, blaming others, and feeling powerless, and examine how these symptoms impact decision-making, problem-solving, and motivation.

**Symptoms of Victim Mentality**

Victim mentality is characterized by several hallmark symptoms that reinforce feelings of helplessness and perpetual dissatisfaction. These symptoms create a mindset that perpetuates a cycle of negative thinking and behaviour, affecting how individuals perceive and interact with the world around them.

1.  **Self-Pity**

Self-pity is one of the most defining characteristics of victim mentality. It involves an excessive focus on one's own misfortunes, often accompanied by feelings of sadness, hopelessness, and the desire for sympathy from others. People who engage in self-pity constantly dwell on their problems and hardships, viewing them as unfair burdens that they are forced to endure.

Self-pity can manifest in many ways, such as frequently complaining about life's difficulties, feeling overwhelmed by minor setbacks, or seeking constant reassurance and validation from others. This mindset traps individuals in a cycle of negativity, where they become preoccupied with their perceived suffering rather than seeking solutions.

For example, someone who frequently says, "Why does this always happen to me?" or "I can't catch a break," is engaging in self-pity. This focus on one's own hardships prevents the person from taking proactive steps to improve their situation, as they become fixated on what is wrong rather than what they can change.

## 2. **Blaming Others**

Blaming others is another common symptom of victim mentality. Individuals with this mindset often deflect responsibility for their problems, pointing the finger at external factors such as other people, circumstances, or bad luck. This behaviour serves as a defence mechanism that protects them from facing uncomfortable truths about their own role in their difficulties.

Blaming others can manifest in both personal and professional settings. In relationships, a person with a victim mentality might blame their partner for their unhappiness, believing that if only the other person changed, everything would be better. At work, they might blame colleagues or management for their lack of progress, failing to recognize their own contribution to the situation.

For instance, an employee who consistently misses deadlines might blame their workload, their boss's expectations, or the behaviour of their coworkers, rather than considering their own time management skills. This deflection of responsibility not only hinders personal growth but also damages relationships, as it creates an environment of conflict and resentment.

### 3. Feeling Powerless

A pervasive sense of powerlessness is at the core of victim mentality. Individuals who feel powerless believe that they have little to no control over their lives, viewing themselves as passive recipients of whatever life throws at them. This mindset leads to a lack of initiative, as the individual assumes that no matter what they do, it won't make a difference.

Feeling powerless often leads to inaction, procrastination, and a tendency to give up easily when faced with challenges. This symptom is closely linked to learned helplessness, a psychological state where repeated exposure to negative experiences teaches the individual that their actions are futile. Over time, this belief becomes deeply ingrained, leading to chronic apathy and a lack of motivation to change.

An example of powerlessness might be someone who consistently says, "There's nothing I can do about it," when faced with a problem, even when there are potential solutions available. This mindset prevents them from exploring options or taking steps to improve their situation, reinforcing the belief that they are forever stuck.

## Impact of Victim Mentality on Decision-Making, Problem-Solving, and Motivation

The symptoms of victim mentality—self-pity, blaming others, and feeling powerless—profoundly affect decision-making, problem-solving, and motivation. These cognitive and emotional patterns create a mental framework that influences every aspect of an individual's life, often leading to choices and behaviours that reinforce the cycle of victimhood.

### 1. Impact on Decision-Making

Victim mentality significantly impairs decision-making by fostering fear, indecision, and a reliance on external validation.

People trapped in this mindset often struggle to make choices, as they are paralyzed by the fear of making the wrong decision. They may hesitate to take risks or try new things because they anticipate failure, rejection, or criticism.

This fear-based approach to decision-making often leads to a pattern of avoidance. Instead of actively pursuing their goals, individuals with a victim mentality may delay decisions or opt for the safest, least challenging path. For instance, someone who feels powerless in their job might avoid applying for a promotion or switching careers, convinced that they will fail no matter what they do.

Moreover, when decisions are made, they are often based on the desire to avoid pain rather than to achieve a positive outcome. This can lead to settling for less, compromising on personal values, or making choices that do not align with one's true desires. The individual becomes stuck in a loop of low expectations and self-fulfilling prophecies, reinforcing their belief that they are destined to struggle.

## 2. Impact on Problem-Solving

Victim mentality severely undermines problem-solving abilities by shifting the focus from solutions to blame. Instead of viewing problems as challenges to be overcome, individuals with this mindset see them as further evidence of their misfortune. This perspective discourages creative thinking and prevents individuals from seeking alternative solutions.

When faced with a problem, someone with a victim mentality might immediately assume there is nothing they can do to change the situation. For example, if a project at work encounters an obstacle, a person with a victim mindset might focus solely on what went wrong and who is to blame, rather than brainstorming ways to resolve the issue. This reactive approach prevents forward momentum, as the individual becomes mired in complaints rather than action.

Furthermore, the habit of blaming others creates a toxic dynamic in team settings, as it fosters conflict and erodes trust. Instead of collaborating to find a solution, the victim mindset encourages finger-pointing and defensiveness, which can derail progress and damage relationships.

3. **Impact on Motivation**

Motivation is often one of the first casualties of victim mentality. The belief that one is powerless or constantly mistreated saps the drive to set and pursue goals. When someone feels that their efforts will inevitably lead to failure or disappointment, it becomes difficult to muster the energy or enthusiasm needed to take action.

This lack of motivation is compounded by the emotional toll of constant self-pity and blame. When an individual is perpetually focused on their perceived misfortunes, they have little mental or emotional bandwidth left for positive pursuits. The resulting apathy leads to a cycle of inaction and regret, further entrenching the victim mentality.

For instance, a person who feels powerless in their personal life might stop setting goals or striving for self-improvement, believing that any effort will be wasted. This resignation to a stagnant status quo prevents them from exploring their potential, achieving their dreams, or finding fulfilment.

### Examples of Victim Mentality in Everyday Scenarios

Victim mentality can manifest in countless ways in everyday life, often influencing interactions, decisions, and self-perception. Here are some common scenarios that illustrate how this mindset plays out in daily situations:

1. **Workplace Conflicts:**

   Imagine an employee named Sarah who frequently feels undervalued at work. When her manager gives her constructive feedback, she immediately interprets it as a personal attack, thinking, "My boss doesn't like me, and no one appreciates my hard work." Instead of seeing the feedback as an opportunity to improve, Sarah feels wronged and resentful, blaming her manager for her lack of progress.

This perception leads Sarah to disengage from her work, putting in minimal effort and avoiding additional responsibilities. She becomes increasingly dissatisfied but does not take steps to address the underlying issues, such as seeking clarification on expectations or asking for professional development opportunities. Her victim mentality keeps her stuck, feeling powerless to change her situation while blaming her manager and colleagues for her unhappiness.

2. **Relationship Challenges**:

John often feels misunderstood and unappreciated by his partner, believing that he always puts in more effort than he receives in return. When conflicts arise, John's first response is to blame his partner, thinking, "If only they were more considerate, we wouldn't have these problems." This mindset prevents him from acknowledging his role in the relationship dynamics or considering his partner's perspective.

John's habit of blaming others and feeling sorry for himself leads to frequent arguments and emotional distance. He feels powerless to improve the relationship, convinced that his partner is the source of all their problems. Instead of working together to find solutions, John's victim mentality keeps him stuck in a loop of resentment and self-pity, eroding the bond he shares with his partner.

3. **Social Interactions**:

Emily often feels excluded and overlooked by her friends. When she sees photos of them socializing without her on social media, she immediately thinks, "They don't care about me. I'm always left out." This belief fuels her self-pity, and she withdraws further, avoiding social events and not reaching out to her friends.

Rather than addressing her feelings or expressing her concerns, Emily blames her friends for her loneliness and isolates herself even more. Her victim mentality prevents her from recognizing that her withdrawal is contributing to the very outcome she fears. Instead of fostering connections, her negative beliefs keep her locked in a cycle of isolation and sadness.

## Conclusion

Recognizing the symptoms of victim mentality—self-pity, blaming others, and feeling powerless—is essential for breaking free from this debilitating mindset. These symptoms not only distort perception and impede decision-making but also sabotage problem-solving efforts and drain motivation. By understanding how victim mentality manifests in everyday scenarios, individuals can begin to identify these patterns in their own lives and take steps to challenge and change them.

The journey to overcoming victim mentality starts with awareness. By acknowledging the impact of these symptoms, individuals can start to reclaim control over their thoughts, actions, and ultimately, their lives. This process involves shifting the focus from blame to responsibility, from self-pity to self-empowerment, and from feeling powerless to taking proactive steps toward change.

# Chapter 4:

# The Impact of Victim Mentality on Personal Life

Victim mentality can profoundly affect personal life, infiltrating every aspect of an individual's thoughts, feelings, and behaviours. This mindset leads to a persistent sense of helplessness, where one sees themselves as a passive recipient of life's hardships rather than an active participant in their own destiny. The consequences of victim mentality extend far beyond day-to-day frustrations; it undermines self-esteem, erodes confidence, and stunts personal growth. In this chapter, we will explore how victim mentality affects personal life, delve into common behaviours like procrastination, avoiding responsibility, and self-sabotage, and examine the long-term impact on mental health, including anxiety and depression.

## How Victim Mentality Affects Self-Esteem, Confidence, and Personal Growth

Victim mentality directly impacts self-esteem and confidence, creating a self-perpetuating cycle where negative beliefs and feelings about oneself become deeply entrenched. At its core, victim mentality convinces individuals that they are powerless to change their circumstances, leading to a diminished sense of self-worth and a lack of belief in their own abilities.

1.  **Impact on Self-Esteem**

    Self-esteem, the value and respect one has for oneself, is heavily influenced by one's thoughts and beliefs. When someone views themselves as a victim, they often internalize negative experiences as personal failures, reinforcing the idea that they are inherently flawed or unworthy. This mindset leads to low self-esteem, as individuals focus on their perceived shortcomings and weaknesses rather than their strengths.

For example, someone with a victim mentality may think, "I'm not good enough," or "I always mess things up," after encountering a setback. These self-critical thoughts become the narrative they live by, preventing them from recognizing their accomplishments or potential. The more they dwell on these negative beliefs, the more their self-esteem deteriorates, making it increasingly difficult to see themselves in a positive light.

Low self-esteem further perpetuates victim mentality because it keeps individuals stuck in a cycle of self-doubt and fear. Instead of taking risks or trying new things, they remain confined within their comfort zones, too afraid to fail or face rejection. This reluctance to step outside of familiar patterns stifles personal growth and keeps them from achieving their goals.

## 2. Impact on Confidence

Confidence, the belief in one's ability to succeed, is another casualty of victim mentality. When individuals constantly view themselves as powerless, they lose the confidence needed to pursue their ambitions and face challenges head-on. This lack of confidence manifests in various ways, including hesitancy to make decisions, reluctance to take on new opportunities, and an overall sense of inadequacy.

For instance, a person with low confidence might avoid applying for a job they want, fearing they will not be good enough or that they will be rejected. This avoidance reinforces their belief that they are not capable, creating a self-fulfilling prophecy where they never give themselves the chance to succeed. The longer this pattern continues, the more their confidence erodes, and the harder it becomes to break free from the cycle of self-doubt.

Without confidence, personal growth stalls. The individual becomes stuck in a loop of safe, familiar behaviours that do not challenge them or push them toward their potential. They may settle for less than they deserve, convinced that they are not worthy of more, and avoid situations that could lead to personal development.

3. **Impact on Personal Growth**

Personal growth requires a willingness to face challenges, take risks, and learn from mistakes. However, victim mentality hinders this process by fostering a mindset that views challenges as threats rather than opportunities. Instead of seeing setbacks as a natural part of growth, individuals with a victim mentality see them as proof of their inadequacy, leading them to avoid difficult situations altogether.

This avoidance behaviour stifles personal growth, as the individual misses valuable learning experiences that could help them develop new skills, build resilience, and gain confidence. They may shy away from pursuing their dreams, settling for a life that feels safe but ultimately unfulfilling. Over time, the lack of growth can lead to feelings of stagnation, frustration, and regret, as the individual realizes they have not lived up to their potential.

## Common Behaviours: Procrastination, Avoiding Responsibility, and Self-Sabotage

Victim mentality often manifests in specific behaviours that further undermine personal success and fulfilment. These behaviours, such as procrastination, avoiding responsibility, and self-sabotage, create barriers to progress and contribute to a cycle of failure and disappointment.

1. **Procrastination**

   Procrastination is a common behaviour among individuals with a victim mentality. It involves delaying tasks or decisions, often due to fear of failure, anxiety, or a lack of motivation. Procrastination provides a temporary escape from uncomfortable feelings, allowing the individual to avoid facing challenges or taking action.

   For someone with a victim mindset, procrastination becomes a way to avoid the perceived pain of making mistakes or being judged. They may tell themselves, "I'll do it later," or "It's not the right time," as a way to justify inaction. However, this delay only leads to increased stress and guilt, reinforcing their negative beliefs about themselves.

   For example, a student who constantly procrastinates on studying may convince themselves that they are simply not good at school, rather than acknowledging their avoidance behaviour. This mindset not only affects their academic performance but also damages their self-esteem, as they repeatedly fall short of their own expectations.

2. **Avoiding Responsibility**

   Avoiding responsibility is another hallmark behaviour of victim mentality. When individuals view themselves as victims, they are quick to shift blame onto others or external circumstances rather than taking ownership of their actions. This deflection of responsibility allows them to avoid the discomfort of acknowledging their role in their problems, but it also prevents them from making meaningful changes.

For instance, someone who is consistently late to work might blame traffic, their alarm clock, or their morning routine, rather than recognizing that they need to better manage their time. By avoiding responsibility, they miss the opportunity to improve their habits and make positive changes in their life.

Avoiding responsibility also impacts relationships, as it creates a dynamic where the individual fails to hold themselves accountable for their actions. This can lead to conflicts, as others may feel frustrated by the constant deflection of blame and lack of effort to resolve issues. Over time, this behaviour erodes trust and damages personal and professional relationships.

3. **Self-Sabotage**

Self-sabotage is a behaviour in which individuals undermine their own success, often unconsciously, due to deeply ingrained fears and negative beliefs. Those with a victim mentality may engage in self-sabotage by setting themselves up for failure, whether through procrastination, neglecting responsibilities, or making poor decisions that conflict with their goals.

Self-sabotage is driven by the belief that one is undeserving of success or incapable of achieving it. For example, someone who fears failure might avoid preparing for a presentation, rationalizing that they were too busy or didn't have enough time. When the presentation goes poorly, they feel validated in their belief that they are not good enough, perpetuating the cycle of self-sabotage.

This behaviour not only prevents personal growth but also reinforces the victim mindset, as the individual continues to see themselves as doomed to fail. Over time, self-sabotage can lead to a deep sense of frustration and disillusionment, as the individual repeatedly falls short of their potential despite their best intentions.

## Long-Term Effects on Mental Health: Anxiety and Depression

The long-term effects of victim mentality on mental health can be severe, often leading to chronic conditions such as anxiety and depression. These mental health issues are exacerbated by the persistent negative thinking patterns, avoidance behaviours, and feelings of helplessness that define victim mentality.

1. **Anxiety**

   Anxiety is a common consequence of victim mentality, as the constant focus on perceived threats, failures, and injustices creates a heightened state of fear and worry. Individuals with a victim mindset are often preoccupied with worst-case scenarios, believing that bad things are bound to happen to them. This fear-based thinking can lead to chronic anxiety, manifesting as excessive worry, restlessness, and difficulty concentrating.

   The impact of anxiety on daily life can be debilitating. It interferes with decision-making, as the individual becomes overwhelmed by the potential negative outcomes of any choice. Anxiety also contributes to avoidance behaviours, as the person tries to minimize their exposure to situations that trigger their fears. This avoidance, however, only serves to reinforce the anxiety, creating a cycle that is difficult to break.

   For example, someone with anxiety driven by a victim mindset might avoid social situations, fearing judgment or rejection. This isolation exacerbates their feelings of loneliness and helplessness, further entrenching their belief that they are a victim of their circumstances.

2. **Depression**

Depression is another common long-term effect of victim mentality. The persistent focus on negative experiences, coupled with feelings of powerlessness and low self-worth, can lead to a profound sense of despair and hopelessness. Individuals with a victim mindset often feel stuck in their circumstances, believing that no matter what they do, things will never improve.

Depression can manifest as a lack of interest in activities, fatigue, changes in sleep and appetite, and persistent feelings of sadness or emptiness. This mental state not only diminishes quality of life but also further reinforces the victim mentality, as the individual loses the motivation to take action or seek help.

The self-perpetuating nature of depression makes it particularly challenging for those with a victim mentality to break free from their negative beliefs. Their inner dialogue often includes thoughts like, "What's the point?" or "I'll never be happy," which serve to deepen their sense of hopelessness and keep them trapped in a cycle of despair.

3. **Impact on Overall Well-Being**

The combination of anxiety, depression, and victim mentality creates a toxic environment for overall well-being. Physical health can also be affected, as chronic stress and negative emotions take a toll on the body, leading to issues such as headaches, digestive problems, and weakened immune function.

Additionally, the impact on relationships and daily functioning can lead to further isolation and dissatisfaction. The individual may withdraw from loved ones, neglect self-care, and lose interest in activities that once brought them joy. Over time, the cumulative effects of victim mentality on mental and physical health can severely diminish one's quality of life.

## Conclusion

Victim mentality has a profound impact on personal life, affecting self-esteem, confidence, and the capacity for personal growth. The behaviours associated with this mindset—such as procrastination, avoiding responsibility, and self-sabotage—create barriers to success and fulfilment, trapping individuals in a cycle of negativity and inaction. The long-term effects on mental health, including anxiety and depression, further compound the challenges, making it difficult for individuals to break free from their self-defeating beliefs.

Recognizing the impact of victim mentality on personal life is the first step toward reclaiming control. By understanding how this mindset affects self-perception, decision-making, and mental health, individuals can begin to challenge their negative beliefs and take proactive steps toward change. Embracing personal responsibility, developing self-compassion, and seeking support are key strategies for overcoming victim mentality and building a healthier, more empowered life.

# Chapter 5:

# The Impact of Victim Mentality on Relationships

Victim mentality doesn't just affect the individual; it ripples outward, profoundly impacting relationships with family, friends, and loved ones. This mindset, characterized by seeing oneself as helpless and unfairly treated, distorts communication and creates unhealthy dynamics that strain personal connections. The constant focus on perceived injustices and external blame disrupts the balance of give-and-take essential for healthy relationships. In this chapter, we will explore how a victim mentality strains relationships, examine common patterns of communication such as defensiveness, criticism, and passive-aggressiveness, and delve into the roles of dependency, neediness, and resentment in the breakdown of relationships.

## How Victim Mentality Strains Personal Relationships

Victim mentality can make relationships challenging to maintain because it fosters a negative and often unbalanced dynamic. Those with a victim mindset often see themselves as powerless, and this outlook affects how they interact with others, influencing their expectations, communication, and emotional responses. This mindset can drive a wedge between individuals and their loved ones, making it difficult to build and sustain positive connections.

1. **Shifting Blame and Avoiding Accountability**

One of the most significant ways victim mentality strains relationships is through the constant shifting of blame onto others. When someone perceives themselves as a perpetual victim, they tend to deflect responsibility for their actions, mistakes, or emotions onto those around them. This deflection can lead to frequent arguments and misunderstandings, as the person never fully acknowledges their role in conflicts or issues.

For example, in a friendship, someone with a victim mentality might frequently complain that they are always taken advantage of or that others don't treat them fairly, yet they fail to recognize how their own behaviour—such as not setting boundaries or being overly accommodating—contributes to the dynamic. This lack of self-awareness and accountability can frustrate others, leading to resentment and emotional distance.

## 2.  Creating an Imbalance of Support

Relationships are meant to be reciprocal, with both parties offering support, understanding, and empathy. However, a victim mentality often creates an imbalance where one person is constantly seeking validation, reassurance, and sympathy, without offering the same in return. This dynamic can exhaust friends and family members, who may feel burdened by the constant need to comfort and console the person with a victim mindset.

Over time, this imbalance can cause significant strain. Friends and family may begin to feel that their needs are secondary or ignored altogether, leading to feelings of neglect and resentment. The relationship becomes one-sided, where the focus is almost entirely on managing the emotions and complaints of the person with a victim mentality, rather than on mutual support and connection.

## 3.  Sabotaging Emotional Intimacy

Emotional intimacy is a cornerstone of close relationships, but victim mentality often sabotages this essential component. The constant focus on negative experiences and perceived wrongs can prevent deeper connections from forming, as the individual with a victim mindset may struggle to open up in a healthy, constructive way. Instead of sharing vulnerabilities in a manner that fosters closeness, they might use their struggles to elicit sympathy or manipulate the emotional landscape of the relationship.

This approach can make others feel manipulated or used, rather than genuinely connected. Instead of mutual sharing and support, conversations often centre on grievances and complaints, leaving little room for positive exchanges or emotional growth. This dynamic can erode trust and make relationships feel more like burdens than sources of joy and comfort.

## Patterns of Communication: Defensiveness, Criticism, and Passive-Aggressiveness

Communication plays a crucial role in the health of any relationship, and victim mentality often distorts how individuals express themselves and respond to others. Common communication patterns associated with victim mentality include defensiveness, criticism, and passive-aggressiveness, each of which can create significant barriers to healthy, productive interactions.

### 1. Defensiveness

Defensiveness is a common communication pattern in those with a victim mentality. Feeling attacked or wronged, they are quick to defend their actions, often without considering the other person's perspective. This defensiveness can make constructive conversations nearly impossible, as the individual focuses on justifying their behaviour rather than addressing the issue at hand.

For example, if a friend expresses concern about a recurring issue, the person with a victim mentality might immediately respond with excuses or counter-criticisms, saying things like, "You're always blaming me" or "It's not my fault, you don't

35

understand what I'm going through." This defensive stance shuts down dialogue and prevents any meaningful resolution, as it shifts the focus away from the problem and toward protecting the victim's self-image.

Defensiveness also discourages others from voicing their concerns, as they fear triggering an emotional reaction or escalating the conflict. Over time, this can lead to a breakdown in communication, where important issues go unaddressed and resentment festers beneath the surface.

## 2. Criticism

Criticism is another communication pattern often seen in those with a victim mentality. Feeling mistreated or unappreciated, they may frequently criticize others, pointing out flaws, mistakes, or perceived slights. This criticism often stems from their own sense of insecurity and need to externalize their frustrations, but it can deeply hurt their relationships.

Criticism can take many forms, from direct insults and negative comments to more subtle jabs and passive-aggressive remarks. For example, someone with a victim mentality might frequently complain that their partner never does anything right or that their friends are always letting them down. These criticisms not only damage the self-esteem of those on the receiving end but also create an environment of negativity and hostility that erodes the foundation of the relationship.

Over time, the constant barrage of criticism can lead to emotional withdrawal, as friends and loved ones feel that nothing they do is ever good enough. This withdrawal further isolates the individual with a victim mentality, reinforcing their belief that they are alone and misunderstood.

## 3. Passive-Aggressiveness

Passive-aggressiveness is a hallmark of victim mentality, characterized by indirect expressions of anger, frustration, or resentment. Rather than addressing issues openly, those with a victim mindset may use sarcasm, backhanded compliments, or silent treatment to communicate their displeasure. This indirect approach allows them to avoid direct confrontation while still expressing their negative emotions.

For example, if someone with a victim mentality feels unappreciated, they might respond with a sarcastic remark like, "Oh sure, it's always my fault," instead of directly expressing their feelings. This type of communication confuses others and often leads to misunderstandings, as it masks the true issue and leaves the other person guessing about the underlying problem.

Passive-aggressiveness creates a toxic dynamic in relationships, as it undermines trust and open communication. Instead of working through conflicts in a healthy way, the individual with a victim mentality resorts to manipulation and guilt-tripping, which further alienates their loved ones.

## The Role of Dependency, Neediness, and Resentment in Relationship Breakdowns

Victim mentality fosters dependency and neediness, as individuals with this mindset often rely heavily on others for validation, emotional support, and decision-making. This dependency can create significant strain in relationships, as it places an undue burden on others to manage the victim's emotional needs. Over time, this dynamic can lead to resentment and eventual breakdowns in the relationship.

### 1. Dependency and Neediness

Dependency in relationships occurs when one person relies excessively on another for emotional stability, reassurance, and guidance. Those with a victim mentality often struggle with self-reliance, viewing others as their primary source of support and validation. This dependency can manifest as clinginess, constant need for reassurance, and a reluctance to make decisions without input from others.

For example, a person with a victim mentality might repeatedly seek advice from a friend or partner, second-guessing their own judgment and becoming overly reliant on others' opinions. While seeking support is normal, excessive dependency can overwhelm the other person, who may feel pressured to constantly be the problem-solver or emotional caretaker.

This neediness can suffocate relationships, as the other person may feel drained by the constant demands and lack of reciprocity. Over time, they may pull away, leading the individual with a victim mentality to feel abandoned or betrayed, further reinforcing their belief that they are always let down by others.

## 2. Resentment

Resentment often builds in relationships affected by victim mentality, both on the part of the victim and their loved ones. The individual with a victim mindset may harbour resentment toward others for perceived slights, unmet expectations, or a lack of understanding. This resentment can manifest as bitterness, passive-aggressiveness, or emotional withdrawal, creating a toxic environment that erodes the relationship's foundation.

On the other hand, friends and family members may also develop resentment due to the constant emotional labour required to support someone with a victim mentality. They may feel taken for granted, unappreciated, or burdened by the unbalanced dynamic. This mutual resentment creates a vicious cycle, where both parties feel wronged and misunderstood, further driving them apart.

## 3. Relationship Breakdowns

The culmination of defensiveness, criticism, passive-aggressiveness, dependency, and resentment often leads to the breakdown of relationships. The constant strain of managing a victim mentality can exhaust even the most patient and compassionate loved ones, leading to emotional distance, conflict, and, ultimately, disconnection.

Over time, these negative patterns erode the trust, respect, and mutual support that healthy relationships require. Friendships may end abruptly, family ties may become strained, and romantic relationships may deteriorate into constant arguments or complete emotional withdrawal. The individual with a victim mentality may be left feeling isolated and rejected, further cementing their belief that they are alone in their struggles.

## Conclusion

Victim mentality profoundly impacts relationships, creating patterns of communication and behaviour that strain even the strongest connections. The constant shifting of blame, defensiveness, criticism, and passive-aggressiveness undermine healthy communication and foster an environment of negativity and mistrust. Dependency, neediness, and resentment further complicate these dynamics, leading to emotional exhaustion and, ultimately, the breakdown of relationships.

Recognizing the impact of victim mentality on relationships is crucial for individuals seeking to rebuild healthier, more balanced connections. By addressing these destructive patterns and learning to take responsibility for one's actions and emotions, individuals can begin to shift away from a victim mindset and toward a more empowered and constructive approach to their relationships. Effective communication, self-awareness, and a commitment to personal growth are essential steps in breaking the cycle of victim mentality and fostering positive, fulfilling relationships.

# Chapter 6:

# The Impact of Victim Mentality on Work Life and Career

Victim mentality not only affects personal and social relationships but also extends its influence into professional life, where its impact can be particularly damaging. A workplace is an environment that demands accountability, adaptability, and proactive behaviour—traits that are often in short supply among those who see themselves as victims. This mindset can stifle career growth, limit ambition, and reduce overall job satisfaction, creating a self-perpetuating cycle of missed opportunities and professional dissatisfaction.

In this chapter, we will explore how victim mentality manifests in the workplace, the common behaviours it fosters, and the long-term effects on career progression, job stability, and mental well-being.

## How Victim Mentality Limits Career Growth, Ambition, and Job Satisfaction

Victim mentality fundamentally undermines a person's professional potential by fostering a negative outlook that affects decision-making, performance, and interactions with colleagues. When individuals see themselves as powerless or believe that external forces consistently block their success, they struggle to take initiative, set goals, and pursue opportunities that could enhance their careers.

1. **Lack of Initiative and Ambition**

People with a victim mentality often lack the drive to advance in their careers. Ambition requires a proactive approach—setting goals, taking on challenges, and continuously seeking growth opportunities. However, those trapped in a victim mindset may avoid taking on new responsibilities or pursuing promotions because they fear failure or rejection. Instead of viewing obstacles as opportunities to learn and grow, they see them as insurmountable barriers set in their path by forces beyond their control.

For instance, an employee with a victim mentality might avoid applying for a promotion, believing that their efforts would be wasted because "the company always favours others" or "nothing ever goes their way." This lack of ambition not only stifles their career progression but also reinforces their belief that success is unattainable.

2. **Low Job Satisfaction**

Victim mentality contributes significantly to low job satisfaction. Individuals who perceive themselves as victims often feel unappreciated, undervalued, and unfairly treated at work. They focus on the negatives—perceived slights from supervisors, uncooperative colleagues, or challenging tasks—rather than recognizing the positive aspects of their job.

This negativity can create a sense of dissatisfaction that persists regardless of actual job conditions. Even in supportive work environments, those with a victim mindset are more likely to interpret neutral or positive situations negatively, further fuelling their discontent. This mindset not only diminishes their enjoyment of work but can also lead to decreased motivation, productivity, and engagement.

3. **Resistance to Feedback and Personal Development**

Career growth often hinges on the ability to receive constructive feedback and make adjustments. However, individuals with a victim mentality tend to perceive feedback as personal criticism rather than an opportunity for improvement. This defensive attitude prevents them from learning from their mistakes, making it difficult for them to develop the skills necessary for advancement.

For example, an employee who consistently deflects feedback by blaming external factors—like "the project was doomed from the start" or "my team didn't support me"—misses valuable learning opportunities. Over time, this resistance to growth can stagnate their career, as they fail to develop the competencies needed to take on more significant roles.

## Common Workplace Behaviours: Avoiding Accountability, Resisting Change, and Blaming Others

Victim mentality manifests in specific workplace behaviours that hinder not only personal success but also team dynamics and overall productivity. These behaviours include avoiding accountability, resisting change, and consistently blaming others for setbacks.

1.  **Avoiding Accountability**

    Avoiding accountability is a hallmark of victim mentality in the workplace. When faced with mistakes or failures, individuals with this mindset often refuse to accept responsibility, instead pointing fingers at colleagues, management, or circumstances beyond their control. This behaviour disrupts the collaborative environment needed for effective teamwork and problem-solving.

    For example, if a project falls behind schedule, a person with a victim mentality might insist that they were not given clear instructions or that another department failed to provide necessary support, rather than acknowledging their own role in the delay. This avoidance of responsibility not only frustrates coworkers but also undermines trust and team cohesion.

Over time, avoiding accountability can lead to a reputation for unreliability, making it less likely that others will want to work with the individual or entrust them with important tasks. This perception can significantly limit career advancement opportunities, as managers seek to promote those who demonstrate responsibility and integrity.

## 2. **Resisting Change**

Change is an inevitable part of any workplace, whether it involves new technology, processes, or organizational structures. However, those with a victim mentality often view change as a threat rather than an opportunity. They may resist new initiatives, complaining that changes are unfair or too difficult, and they often focus on what could go wrong instead of the potential benefits.

For instance, when a company implements a new software system, an employee with a victim mindset might resist learning it, citing reasons such as "I'm not good with technology" or "This is just going to make everything harder." This resistance not only hampers their performance but also creates friction within the team, as others have to compensate for their reluctance to adapt.

Resisting change can lead to stagnation and a lack of skill development, making it difficult for the individual to stay relevant in a rapidly evolving job market. It also positions them as a negative influence in the workplace, further damaging their professional reputation and relationships.

## 3. **Blaming Others**

Blaming others is a common defence mechanism for those with a victim mentality. In the workplace, this behaviour manifests as a refusal to take ownership of one's actions, leading to conflicts with colleagues and supervisors. This blame-shifting not only alienates coworkers but also disrupts the problem-solving process, as energy is wasted on assigning fault rather than finding solutions.

For example, if a team project fails to meet its goals, an individual with a victim mindset might blame their coworkers for not pulling their weight or accuse their manager of poor leadership, rather than reflecting on how they could have contributed differently. This blame game creates a toxic work environment, where collaboration is hindered by mistrust and resentment.

Over time, blaming others can erode professional relationships and damage the individual's credibility. Colleagues and supervisors may come to view them as difficult to work with, reducing opportunities for collaboration, mentorship, and career growth.

## Long-Term Career Impacts: Missed Opportunities, Burnout, and Job Instability

The long-term effects of victim mentality on work life can be severe, often leading to missed opportunities, burnout, and job instability. These outcomes not only hinder professional success but also contribute to ongoing cycles of dissatisfaction and negative self-perception.

1. **Missed Opportunities**

   Victim mentality often leads to missed opportunities for career advancement, professional development, and personal growth. When individuals consistently view themselves as powerless or unfairly treated, they are less likely to take risks, seek out new challenges, or advocate for themselves in the workplace. This hesitation can result in a stagnant career path, where promotions, raises, and other opportunities for advancement pass them by.

For example, someone with a victim mindset might decline to apply for a leadership position, fearing that they would not be supported or that the odds are stacked against them. Even when opportunities are presented, they may lack the confidence or motivation to pursue them, believing that their efforts will ultimately be futile.

This pattern of missed opportunities compounds over time, leading to a career that feels unfulfilling and stagnant. As their peers advance, those with a victim mentality may feel increasingly left behind, reinforcing their sense of helplessness and resignation.

2. **Burnout**

Burnout is a significant risk for individuals with a victim mentality, as the constant focus on perceived injustices and negative experiences creates a cycle of stress and exhaustion. In the workplace, this mindset can make even routine tasks feel overwhelming, as every setback is seen as further evidence of their inability to succeed.

The emotional toll of victim mentality—constant anxiety, frustration, and feelings of inadequacy—can quickly lead to burnout. This burnout not only reduces job performance and productivity but also has serious implications for mental and physical health. Individuals may experience symptoms such as chronic fatigue, difficulty concentrating, and increased absenteeism, further jeopardizing their career stability.

Burnout also diminishes job satisfaction, making it difficult for individuals to find joy or purpose in their work. This lack of fulfilment can lead to disengagement, poor performance, and ultimately, the decision to leave the job, either voluntarily or as a result of termination.

3. **Job Instability**

The behaviours associated with victim mentality—avoiding accountability, resisting change, and blaming others—can lead to job instability over time. When these patterns persist, they can erode professional relationships, diminish job performance, and create a negative reputation that follows the individual from one job to the next.

Job instability might manifest as frequent job changes, periods of unemployment, or difficulty securing promotions or stable positions. The individual's reluctance to take responsibility and adapt to new situations makes them a less attractive candidate for employers, who value reliability, adaptability, and a proactive approach.

Moreover, job instability reinforces the individual's sense of victimhood, as each setback or job loss is perceived as further proof that the world is against them. This cycle of instability can be difficult to break, as it perpetuates the very mindset that created it.

## Conclusion

Victim mentality has a profound and far-reaching impact on work life and career. It limits ambition, reduces job satisfaction, and fosters behaviours that disrupt professional success, such as avoiding accountability, resisting change, and blaming others. Over time, these patterns lead to missed opportunities, burnout, and job instability, creating a self-fulfilling cycle of professional dissatisfaction and career stagnation.

Recognizing the impact of victim mentality on one's work life is a crucial step toward change. By challenging self-defeating thoughts, taking responsibility for actions, and embracing opportunities for growth, individuals can begin to break free from the constraints of a victim mindset. Cultivating a proactive, empowered approach to work not only enhances career prospects but also contributes to a more fulfilling and balanced professional life.

# Chapter 7:

# The Cycle of Self-Sabotage in Victim Mentality

Victim mentality is not just a passive state of feeling wronged or helpless; it actively shapes a person's behaviour in ways that can be profoundly self-destructive. At the core of this mindset lies a cycle of self-sabotage—a repetitive pattern of negative thoughts, fear of failure, avoidance, and actions that undermine personal and professional success. This cycle can feel like a trap, where every attempt at progress is met with internal resistance, reinforcing feelings of inadequacy and helplessness.

In this chapter, we will explore in detail how victim mentality fosters self-sabotage, the psychological connections between fear of failure, avoidance, and low self-worth, and provide real-life examples of how these destructive behaviours manifest in work, relationships, and personal goals.

## How Victim Mentality and Negative Thoughts Create a Cycle of Self-Sabotage

Self-sabotage is the act of undermining one's own efforts, often unconsciously, through behaviours that prevent achieving desired goals. For individuals with a victim mentality, this pattern of self-destruction is driven by deeply ingrained negative beliefs about themselves and the world around them.

1.  **The Role of Negative Thoughts in Self-Sabotage**

Negative thinking is a defining characteristic of victim mentality and a major driver of self-sabotage. Individuals with this mindset constantly engage in self-defeating thought patterns that emphasize their perceived inability to overcome obstacles. Thoughts like "I'll never be good enough," "Nothing ever works out for me," or "There's no point in trying because I'll fail anyway" create a powerful psychological barrier that makes even the smallest step forward seem insurmountable.

These negative thoughts not only shape how people see themselves but also dictate their actions—or lack thereof. By constantly dwelling on their perceived limitations, individuals with a victim mentality set themselves up for failure before they even begin. They anticipate negative outcomes, and in an effort to protect themselves from the pain of failure or rejection, they engage in behaviours that ultimately ensure those outcomes come true.

2. **Fear of Failure and Avoidance**

Fear of failure is a fundamental aspect of self-sabotage for those with a victim mentality. Because they see failure not just as a setback but as a reflection of their inherent unworthiness, the prospect of failing is terrifying. This fear leads to avoidance behaviours—procrastination, indecision, and an unwillingness to take risks. By avoiding situations where failure is possible, they temporarily protect themselves from immediate disappointment but, in doing so, deny themselves the opportunity for success.

For example, someone with a victim mentality may delay starting a new project at work, not because they are lazy, but because they are afraid that their efforts will not be good enough. The avoidance provides a short-term escape from the anxiety of potential failure, but it also ensures that they miss deadlines, deliver subpar work, or never complete the task at all, reinforcing their belief that they are incapable.

3. **Low Self-Worth and Self-Sabotage**

At the heart of the cycle of self-sabotage lies low self-worth. Individuals with a victim mentality often feel unworthy of success, happiness, or recognition. This deeply held belief fuels behaviours that keep them stuck in a pattern of self-destruction. Even when opportunities for positive change arise, their sense of unworthiness can cause them to unconsciously undermine their own efforts.

For instance, someone with low self-worth may receive praise for their work but immediately downplay it, thinking, "They're just being nice; I don't deserve it." This self-deprecating mindset can lead them to reject opportunities for advancement, shy away from recognition, or fail to advocate for themselves. In doing so, they reinforce their own negative self-image, perpetuating the cycle of self-sabotage.

## Real-Life Examples of Self-Sabotage in Work, Relationships, and Personal Goals

Self-sabotage manifests in various aspects of life, including work, relationships, and personal goals. These behaviours are often subtle and insidious, making them difficult to recognize until their impact becomes undeniable.

### 1. Self-Sabotage in Work

In the workplace, self-sabotage can manifest as procrastination, underperformance, and conflict avoidance. A person with a victim mentality might consistently miss deadlines, not because they lack the skills, but because they are overwhelmed by self-doubt and fear of failing. Their negative thoughts paralyze them, leading to avoidance and last-minute rushes that almost guarantee a poor outcome.

For example, an employee may be fully capable of excelling in their role, but their constant fear of making mistakes causes them to second-guess every decision. They spend excessive time ruminating on what could go wrong, delaying actions that could lead to success. This procrastination often results in missed opportunities, poor evaluations, and a lack of career progression, all of which reinforce the belief that they are destined to fail.

Additionally, self-sabotage at work can include avoiding feedback or constructive criticism. An employee with a victim mentality might avoid asking for feedback on their performance, fearing criticism will confirm their worst fears about themselves. This avoidance not only stunts their professional growth but also limits their ability to improve and excel in their role.

## 2. Self-Sabotage in Relationships

In personal relationships, self-sabotage often appears as defensiveness, withdrawal, and an inability to communicate effectively. Those with a victim mentality may feel unworthy of love and affection, leading them to push people away or test the limits of their relationships. They may unconsciously create drama or conflict, driven by the belief that it's only a matter of time before they are let down or hurt.

For example, someone who feels unworthy of love might react to their partner's attempts at closeness with suspicion or criticism, constantly seeking evidence that they will be abandoned or betrayed. This behaviour can drive partners away, reinforcing the self-fulfilling prophecy that they are destined to be alone.

Another common form of self-sabotage in relationships is dependency. Feeling powerless and incapable of managing their own emotions, individuals with a victim mentality may cling excessively to their partners, placing unrealistic demands on them to provide constant reassurance and support. This neediness can overwhelm their partners, leading to tension and eventual breakdowns in the relationship.

## 3. Self-Sabotage in Personal Goals

Self-sabotage also extends to personal goals and aspirations, where fear of failure, procrastination, and perfectionism prevent individuals from making meaningful progress. Those with a victim mentality may set goals for themselves—such as losing weight, learning a new skill, or starting a new project—but struggle to follow through, paralyzed by their own negative expectations.

For instance, someone might set a goal to get in shape but repeatedly skip workouts because they feel they're too out of shape to even start. They tell themselves, "What's the point? I'll never be fit anyway," and give up before they've even begun. This cycle of setting and abandoning goals not only keeps them stuck but also erodes their self-confidence, further entrenching the belief that they are incapable of change.

Similarly, perfectionism—a common trait among those with a victim mentality—can lead to self-sabotage by setting impossibly high standards that are nearly impossible to meet. Fear of not being perfect can cause them to delay starting projects, over-edit their work, or never complete tasks, ensuring that they never achieve the success they desire.

**Breaking the Cycle of Self-Sabotage**

Breaking the cycle of self-sabotage requires a conscious effort to recognize and challenge the negative thoughts and beliefs that drive self-destructive behaviours. It involves developing self-awareness, practicing self-compassion, and taking small, consistent steps toward change.

1. **Recognizing Negative Thought Patterns**

The first step in breaking the cycle is to become aware of the negative thought patterns that fuel self-sabotage. This means paying attention to the internal dialogue that occurs when faced with challenges, opportunities, or feedback. By identifying thoughts like "I can't do this" or "I'm not good enough," individuals can start to challenge and reframe these beliefs.

2. **Challenging Fear of Failure**

Addressing the fear of failure is crucial in overcoming self-sabotage. Rather than viewing failure as a reflection of their worth, individuals need to reframe it as a learning opportunity. This shift in perspective can reduce the fear that paralyzes action, making it easier to take risks and pursue goals without the constant dread of not measuring up.

Techniques such as cognitive-behavioural therapy (CBT) or journaling can help individuals confront and reframe their fears, turning them into motivators rather than barriers.

### 3.  Building Self-Worth

Developing self-worth is a key component of breaking free from self-sabotage. This involves learning to value oneself independently of external validation and recognizing that worthiness is not contingent on success or failure. Practices like affirmations, self-compassion exercises, and setting realistic, attainable goals can help build a more positive self-image.

### 4.  Taking Small Steps Toward Change

Finally, breaking the cycle of self-sabotage involves taking small, manageable steps toward change. Rather than setting overwhelming goals that trigger fear and avoidance, individuals can focus on incremental progress. This approach helps build confidence and momentum, gradually shifting the mindset from "I can't" to "I can."

Celebrating small victories, learning from setbacks, and maintaining a focus on progress rather than perfection can help individuals move beyond self-sabotage and toward a more empowered and fulfilling life.

## Conclusion

The cycle of self-sabotage in victim mentality is a deeply ingrained pattern of negative thoughts, fear of failure, avoidance, and self-destructive behaviours that affect every aspect of life.

# Living with Victim Mentality

From missed opportunities at work to strained relationships and abandoned personal goals, self-sabotage keeps individuals trapped in a perpetual state of dissatisfaction and helplessness.

Breaking free from this cycle requires courage, self-awareness, and a commitment to challenging the negative beliefs that drive self-sabotaging actions. By taking proactive steps to build self-worth, confront fears, and embrace change, individuals can begin to rewrite their narratives, moving from a mindset of victimhood to one of empowerment and possibility.

# Chapter 8:

# The Role of the Inner Critic

The inner critic is a pervasive and often destructive force that plays a significant role in the development and maintenance of victim mentality. This internal voice is constantly at work, criticizing, doubting, and belittling an individual's every move, reinforcing the negative thoughts and self-defeating beliefs that fuel the cycle of victimhood. Understanding the inner critic is crucial to breaking free from victim mentality because this voice serves as the gatekeeper of self-perception, shaping how one views themselves and the world around them.

In this chapter, we will explore the role of the inner critic in victim mentality, how it reinforces negative thoughts and self-sabotaging behaviours, and provide techniques to identify, challenge, and quiet this harmful inner voice.

## Understanding the Inner Critic as a Key Driver of Victim Mentality

The inner critic is the voice inside that constantly judges, criticizes, and undermines your self-worth. It often sounds like a harsh, overly critical parent or a disapproving authority figure, constantly reminding you of your perceived shortcomings and failures. This internal dialogue can be relentless, and over time, it becomes a deeply ingrained part of how you see yourself.

### 1. Origins of the Inner Critic

The inner critic often has its roots in early life experiences, such as critical or dismissive parenting, bullying, or trauma. For some, it might have developed as a coping mechanism to help navigate difficult or unpredictable environments. The inner critic is an internalized voice that mirrors the external criticism or rejection experienced in formative years. If you grew up hearing that you weren't good enough, that you constantly failed to meet expectations, or that your efforts were always lacking, these messages can become internalized as part of your self-identity.

For individuals with a victim mentality, the inner critic is not just a nagging voice—it becomes a defining force that shapes how they interact with the world. It tells them that they are powerless, undeserving, and destined to fail. This constant barrage of negativity reinforces the belief that they are perpetual victims of their circumstances, unworthy of success or happiness.

### 2. How the Inner Critic Shapes Self-Perception

The inner critic is a master at distorting reality, twisting facts to fit its narrative of inadequacy and failure. It magnifies mistakes, minimizes successes, and constantly points out flaws, no matter how minor. For someone with a victim mentality, the inner critic becomes a self-fulfilling prophecy—it convinces them that they are helpless, unworthy, and powerless, and they begin to act accordingly.

The inner critic's voice can sound like:

- o "You're never going to be good enough."
- o "Why even try? You'll just fail like you always do."
- o "It's your fault this happened; you always mess things up."
- o "No one likes you; you're just a burden."

These thoughts create a mental environment where every action is second-guessed, every decision is clouded with self-doubt, and every opportunity feels out of reach. This pervasive negativity not only keeps the individual stuck in a victim mindset but also fuels anxiety, depression, and a sense of hopelessness.

## How the Inner Critic Reinforces Negative Thoughts and Self-Defeating Beliefs

The inner critic is not just a passive commentator; it actively shapes behaviour and decision-making. Its influence can be seen in various areas of life, driving self-defeating actions that reinforce victim mentality.

### 1. Perpetuating Self-Blame and Guilt

One of the primary ways the inner critic reinforces victim mentality is through self-blame and guilt. This voice constantly reminds individuals of their past mistakes, emphasizing their role in every negative outcome. Instead of recognizing external factors or circumstances beyond their control, the inner critic convinces them that every failure is a personal failing.

For example, if a relationship ends, the inner critic might say, "It's all your fault. If you were better, they would have stayed." This reinforces feelings of unworthiness and self-blame, preventing the individual from learning from the experience and moving forward. The constant self-blame keeps them trapped in a cycle of regret and hopelessness, unable to see a way out of their perceived failures.

### 2. Magnifying Fear of Failure and Inadequacy

The inner critic amplifies fears of failure and feelings of inadequacy, making it difficult for individuals to take risks or pursue new opportunities. It whispers that any effort is doomed to fail, creating a fear of taking action that can lead to procrastination, avoidance, and ultimately, self-sabotage.

For instance, someone with a victim mentality might avoid applying for a promotion because the inner critic tells them, "You're not qualified. You'll embarrass yourself if you even try." This fear-driven avoidance ensures that they miss out on opportunities for growth, further solidifying the belief that they are stuck and powerless.

### 3. Undermining Self-Confidence and Motivation

The inner critic constantly undermines self-confidence by highlighting perceived flaws and failures, no matter how trivial. Even in moments of success, the inner critic can find a way to twist the narrative, making the accomplishment seem unearned or insignificant.

For example, after completing a challenging project, instead of feeling proud, the inner critic might say, "You only finished it because you got lucky; anyone could have done that." This relentless criticism drains motivation and self-esteem, making it difficult to maintain the energy and drive needed to pursue goals.

### 4. Creating an Overwhelming Sense of Helplessness

Ultimately, the inner critic fosters a deep sense of helplessness. By constantly reinforcing negative beliefs and self-doubt, it convinces individuals that they have no control over their lives. This perceived lack of agency is a hallmark of victim mentality, as the individual feels perpetually trapped by their circumstances with no hope for change.

## Techniques to Identify and Quiet the Inner Critic

Overcoming the inner critic is essential to breaking free from victim mentality. This process involves recognizing the critic's voice, challenging its validity, and replacing its negative messages with more empowering, compassionate thoughts.

### 1. Identifying the Inner Critic's Voice

The first step in quieting the inner critic is learning to recognize when it's speaking. Often, the inner critic's voice is so familiar that it feels like a natural part of one's thought process. However, it is essential to distinguish the critic's voice from your authentic self.

- o **Mindfulness:** Practicing mindfulness can help increase awareness of negative thoughts as they occur. By paying attention to your inner dialogue without judgment, you can start to notice patterns in how the inner critic speaks. For example, notice when you use words like "always," "never," or "should," as these are often signs of the inner critic's influence.
- o **Journaling:** Keeping a thought journal can help you identify the inner critic's patterns. Write down critical thoughts as they occur and review them regularly. This practice can help you see how often and in what situations the inner critic shows up, providing insight into its triggers.

## 2. Challenging the Inner Critic's Beliefs

Once you've identified the inner critic's voice, the next step is to challenge its messages. Remember that the inner critic's statements are not facts; they are distorted interpretations rooted in fear and past experiences.

- o **Question the Evidence:** When the inner critic makes a statement like "You're a failure," ask yourself, "What evidence do I have that this is true? Are there examples that contradict this belief?" By looking at the facts, you can begin to see that the critic's narrative is often exaggerated or entirely false.
- o **Reframe Negative Thoughts:** Instead of accepting the critic's judgment, try to reframe the thought in a more balanced way. For example, if the critic says, "You always mess things up," reframe it as, "I made a mistake, but I've learned from it, and I can do better next time." This approach helps to shift the focus from self-blame to growth and learning.

## 3. Practicing Self-Compassion

A powerful antidote to the inner critic is self-compassion. This involves treating yourself with the same kindness and understanding that you would offer to a friend. Self-compassion allows you to acknowledge your imperfections without judgment and to recognize that making mistakes is a normal part of being human.

- o **Affirmations:** Using positive affirmations can help counteract the inner critic's negativity. Phrases like "I am enough," "I deserve happiness," or "I am capable of overcoming challenges" can help rewire your thinking and build a more compassionate inner dialogue.
- o **Self-Soothing Techniques:** Engage in activities that nurture and comfort you, such as meditation, exercise, or spending time in nature. These practices help to create a more positive internal environment, making it easier to quiet the inner critic.

4. **Creating a Dialogue with the Inner Critic**

Engaging in a dialogue with the inner critic can help you understand its motivations and reduce its power. The inner critic often emerges from a place of fear and protection, albeit misguided. By addressing it directly, you can begin to reframe its influence.

- o **Personify the Critic:** Imagine the inner critic as a separate character or entity. Give it a name, visualize what it might look like, and talk to it as you would another person. This separation allows you to distance yourself from the critic's negativity and see it as something you can challenge, rather than an intrinsic part of who you are.
- o **Set Boundaries:** Just as you would set boundaries with a critical person in your life, set boundaries with your inner critic. When it begins to speak, firmly remind it, "I hear you,

but I'm choosing to think differently." This assertion helps reclaim control over your thoughts.

5. **Seeking Support**

Sometimes, the inner critic's voice is deeply entrenched and overcoming it may require external support. Therapy, particularly cognitive-behavioural therapy (CBT), can be highly effective in helping individuals challenge negative thought patterns and develop healthier ways of thinking.

> o **Therapists and Coaches:** Working with a therapist or coach can provide valuable insights into the origins of your inner critic and offer strategies for managing it. This support can be instrumental in breaking free from victim mentality and building a more empowered sense of self.

**Conclusion**

The inner critic is a key driver of victim mentality, constantly reinforcing negative thoughts, self-doubt, and self-defeating beliefs. By understanding the origins of the inner critic, recognizing its voice, and actively challenging its messages, individuals can begin to break free from its grip. Cultivating self-compassion, setting boundaries with the critic, and seeking support when needed are essential steps in quieting this inner voice and reclaiming a sense of agency and self-worth.

Overcoming the inner critic is not an overnight process, but with persistence and self-awareness, it is possible to transform this harsh voice into a more supportive and encouraging inner dialogue, paving the way for a life free from the constraints of victim mentality.

# Chapter 9:

# Overcoming the Blame Game

Blame is a central feature of victim mentality, acting as a defence mechanism that allows individuals to deflect responsibility and avoid confronting their own role in their challenges. This "blame game" can feel comforting in the short term because it absolves the individual of personal responsibility, but it ultimately perpetuates feelings of helplessness, stagnation, and a lack of control over one's life. To break free from the constraints of victim mentality, it's essential to understand the role of blame, recognize its destructive impact, and learn how to shift from blame to accountability.

This chapter will explore the function of blame in victim mentality, how it undermines personal growth and perpetuates feelings of powerlessness and provide strategies to move from a mindset of blame to one of accountability.

## The Role of Blame in Victim Mentality and How It Deflects Responsibility

Blame is the act of assigning responsibility for a negative event or outcome to someone or something else. For individuals with a victim mentality, blame serves as a way to avoid the discomfort of self-reflection and personal accountability. It externalizes problems, making them about others rather than looking inward and addressing personal contributions to the situation.

1. **Blame as a Defence Mechanism**

Blame functions as a psychological defence mechanism that shields individuals from feelings of guilt, shame, or inadequacy. When something goes wrong, blaming others or external circumstances provides an immediate, albeit temporary, sense of relief. It allows individuals to preserve their self-image by avoiding the painful process of self-examination.

- o **Protection from Vulnerability:** By blaming others, the individual avoids the vulnerability that comes with admitting mistakes or shortcomings. This avoidance can be rooted in deep-seated fears of not being good enough or capable enough.
- o **Justification of Negative Feelings:** Blame justifies negative emotions, such as anger, resentment, or disappointment. For example, "I'm angry because my coworker messed up" shifts the focus away from any personal role in the conflict and places the emotional burden on someone else.

## 2. The Cycle of Deflecting Responsibility

When blame becomes a habitual response, it creates a cycle of deflecting responsibility that reinforces victim mentality. This cycle involves:

- o **Externalizing Problems:** Blame shifts the focus outward, making problems seem like they are caused entirely by other people or uncontrollable circumstances. This leads to a lack of introspection and personal growth.
- o **Avoidance of Action:** By blaming others, individuals avoid taking constructive action to improve their situation. Instead of seeking solutions, they remain stuck in a narrative of powerlessness and injustice.
- o **Reinforcing Powerlessness:** Each time blame is used to deflect responsibility, it reinforces the belief that the individual has no control over

their life. This learned helplessness becomes a self-fulfilling prophecy, as they continue to feel trapped and unable to change their circumstances.

## How Blaming Others Perpetuates Feelings of Helplessness and Stagnation

Blaming others may provide temporary emotional relief, but it ultimately keeps individuals stuck in patterns of helplessness and stagnation. It disconnects them from their own power to effect change, leaving them reliant on external factors to improve their lives.

1.  **Loss of Personal Agency**

Blame strips away personal agency by positioning individuals as passive recipients of life's challenges rather than active participants. When someone consistently blames external forces, they relinquish their ability to make changes. This mindset leads to a feeling of being at the mercy of others, unable to influence outcomes or take control of one's life.

> o   **Examples in Daily Life:** In the workplace, an employee who blames their manager for lack of progress might stop putting in effort, believing that no matter what they do, their contributions will go unnoticed. In relationships, someone who blames their partner for ongoing issues might avoid having difficult conversations or making necessary changes, believing it's the other person's responsibility to fix things.

2.  **Stagnation in Personal Growth**

Blame hinders personal growth by preventing individuals from learning from their mistakes and challenges. When problems are always someone else's fault, there is no impetus to reflect, adapt, or change. This lack of self-awareness stunts emotional and psychological development, leading to repeated patterns of behaviour and persistent dissatisfaction.

- o **Reinforcing Negative Beliefs:** Blaming others reinforces negative beliefs about oneself and the world. Statements like "Nothing ever goes my way because people are always against me" perpetuate a narrative of victimhood, ensuring that the individual remains trapped in a cycle of negativity.

3. **Damaging Relationships**

Blame is corrosive to relationships, creating conflict and resentment. It fosters a dynamic where one person is always at fault, leading to defensiveness and breakdowns in communication. Over time, this can erode trust and intimacy, pushing people away and reinforcing the victim's sense of isolation.

- o **Patterns of Communication:** In relationships, the constant use of blame can manifest as criticism, stonewalling, and refusal to take ownership of one's actions. This creates a toxic environment where issues are never fully addressed or resolved, leading to ongoing tension and unhappiness.

4. **Perpetuation of Learned Helplessness**

Learned helplessness is a state where individuals feel powerless to change their situation, often because they have been conditioned to believe that their actions have no impact. Blame is a key factor in this conditioning, as it continually externalizes control and reinforces the belief that the individual is incapable of making meaningful changes.

- o **Impact on Motivation:** When someone believes that others are always to blame, they lose motivation to try new things or put in effort to improve their situation. This leads to a lack of initiative and a passive approach to life, where opportunities are missed, and growth is stunted.

**Strategies to Shift from Blame to Accountability**

Breaking the cycle of blame requires a conscious shift toward accountability—taking responsibility for one's actions, choices, and their consequences. Accountability is not about self-blame or accepting fault for everything but about recognizing one's power to influence outcomes and make proactive changes.

1.  **Self-Reflection and Ownership**

The first step in moving from blame to accountability is self-reflection. This involves examining your role in a situation and acknowledging where you might have contributed to the problem. It's about taking ownership of your actions without self-condemnation.

 - o **Ask Reflective Questions:** When faced with a challenging situation, ask yourself, "What role did I play in this? What could I have done differently? How can I take responsibility for my actions moving forward?" These questions encourage introspection and help shift the focus from external blame to internal accountability.
 - o **Identify Patterns:** Look for recurring patterns in your behaviour that contribute to the problems you face. For example, if you often find yourself in conflicts, reflect on your communication style and how it might be affecting your interactions. Recognizing these patterns is the first step in breaking them.

2.  **Reframing Blame as Learning Opportunities**

Reframing blame as an opportunity for learning and growth allows you to see mistakes not as failures but as valuable lessons.

Instead of focusing on who is at fault, shift your mindset to what can be learned from the situation.

- **Adopt a Growth Mindset:** A growth mindset is the belief that abilities and intelligence can be developed through effort, learning, and perseverance. Embracing this mindset encourages you to view setbacks as opportunities for growth rather than reasons to blame others.
- **Focus on Solutions, Not Fault:** When confronted with a problem, instead of asking, "Who caused this?" ask, "What can I do to improve this situation?" This approach shifts the conversation from blame to action, empowering you to take control and make positive                                    changes.

3. **Practice Empathy and Understanding**

Blame often arises from a lack of empathy and a focus on one's own perspective. By practicing empathy, you can better understand the viewpoints of others and see the situation more holistically.

- **Put Yourself in Others' Shoes:** Before assigning blame, consider the other person's perspective. What challenges might they be facing? How might their actions be influenced by factors you're unaware of? This shift in perspective can reduce blame and foster a more collaborative approach to problem-solving.
- **Communicate Openly and Honestly:** Open communication helps to address issues without falling into the blame trap. Express your feelings and needs without accusing or attacking others. For example, instead of saying, "You always make me feel ignored," try saying, "I feel unheard when our conversations are one-sided,

and I would appreciate more engagement."

## 4. Develop Personal Responsibility Habits

Building habits of personal responsibility helps to cultivate a sense of agency and control over your life. These habits reinforce the idea that while you cannot control everything, you can always control your response and actions.

- o **Set Personal Goals:** Setting goals gives you a sense of direction and purpose. By working toward these goals, you take active steps to shape your future, reducing the inclination to blame external factors when things don't go as planned.
- o **Accountability Partners:** Engage with accountability partners—people who can help you stay on track and provide honest feedback. This could be a friend, coach, or mentor who encourages you to take responsibility and supports you in your growth journey.

## 5. Challenge the "Blame Narrative"

The "blame narrative" is the internal story that attributes your problems to others or circumstances. To overcome it, actively challenge this narrative by questioning its accuracy and reframing it in a more balanced way.

- o **Rewrite the Story:** When you catch yourself blaming, pause and rewrite the narrative. For example, change "I failed because my boss didn't support me" to "I didn't get the support I expected, but I can still find ways to succeed." This subtle shift empowers you to take action and move forward.

## Conclusion

Blame is a powerful, yet ultimately destructive, element of victim mentality. It deflects responsibility, reinforces helplessness, and keeps individuals trapped in cycles of stagnation and resentment. By shifting from blame to accountability, individuals can reclaim their power, take control of their actions, and create positive changes in their personal and professional lives.

Embracing accountability is not about accepting fault for everything but about recognizing your role in your experiences and making proactive choices that lead to growth and fulfilment. With self-reflection, empathy, and a commitment to personal responsibility, it is possible to overcome the blame game and build a more empowered and resilient mindset.

# Chapter 10:

# The Cost of Staying Stuck

Remaining trapped in a victim mindset comes with significant costs that affect every aspect of an individual's life. While it may seem easier or safer to stay in familiar patterns of blaming, self-pity, and avoidance, the long-term consequences can be devastating. This chapter delves into the emotional, financial, and social costs of maintaining a victim mentality, highlighting how staying stuck leads to missed opportunities, unfulfilled potential, and a deteriorating quality of life. It also examines the profound impact that a victim mindset can have on physical health and overall well-being.

## The Emotional Cost of Staying Stuck

One of the most immediate and profound costs of a victim mentality is the emotional toll it takes on an individual. Living in a constant state of blame, helplessness, and resentment creates a deeply negative emotional environment that can undermine mental health and well-being.

### 1. Chronic Stress and Anxiety

Staying stuck in a victim mindset often means living in a constant state of stress and anxiety. When you perceive yourself as powerless, life feels unpredictable and overwhelming, leading to heightened emotional arousal.

    o   **The Cycle of Worry:** The belief that you have no control over your circumstances perpetuates a cycle of worry and fear. This chronic stress response affects your body's nervous system, keeping you in a heightened state of alertness that is mentally and physically exhausting.

o **Anxiety and Overthinking:** A victim mentality often involves ruminating over past injustices or perceived threats. This overthinking creates a sense of doom and leads to anxiety, making even simple decisions feel daunting.

2. **Depression and Hopelessness**

The emotional burden of victim mentality can lead to depression. When you feel trapped in negative circumstances with no perceived way out, hopelessness sets in. Depression is often fuelled by feelings of unworthiness, self-blame, and a pervasive sense of failure, all of which are hallmarks of victim mentality.

o **Loss of Motivation:** Depression saps motivation and energy, making it hard to engage in activities that could improve your situation. This lack of motivation reinforces the cycle of stagnation and victimhood, creating a self-perpetuating loop of despair.

o **Emotional Numbness:** Over time, the emotional pain of living as a victim can lead to numbness, where you disconnect from both positive and negative feelings. This emotional shutdown serves as a coping mechanism but ultimately results in a diminished quality of life.

3. **Low Self-Esteem and Self-Worth**

Victim mentality erodes self-esteem and self-worth. When you see yourself as someone to whom bad things happen, it's difficult to maintain a positive self-image. This low self-esteem not only affects how you see yourself but also how you allow others to treat you.

- o **Negative Self-Talk:** The constant inner dialogue of self-criticism, self-blame, and unworthiness reinforces feelings of inadequacy. Over time, this negative self-talk can become a deeply ingrained belief that shapes every decision and action.
- o **Fear of Rejection and Failure:** Low self-worth often leads to a fear of taking risks or trying new things. The fear of rejection or failure becomes overwhelming, keeping you stuck in a comfort zone that, ironically, is far from comfortable.

**The Financial Cost of Staying Stuck**

Victim mentality also carries significant financial implications. By avoiding responsibility and accountability, individuals often miss opportunities for career growth, financial stability, and personal success.

1. **Missed Career Opportunities**

Victim mentality limits ambition and inhibits professional growth. When you constantly blame others for your lack of progress, you miss opportunities to advance in your career. This mindset creates a barrier to success, as it discourages proactive behaviour and fosters a defeatist attitude.

- o **Stagnation in the Workplace:** Blaming coworkers, managers, or organizational structures for your lack of success keeps you from seeking promotions, learning new skills, or taking on new challenges. This stagnation not only limits your income potential but also reduces job satisfaction and engagement.
- o **Avoidance of Responsibility:** In the workplace, a victim mentality often manifests as avoidance of responsibility. Instead of taking ownership of tasks or seeking out leadership roles, individuals with this mindset shy away

from challenges, further hindering their professional development.

## 2. Poor Financial Decisions

The emotional toll of victim mentality can lead to poor financial decision-making. Feelings of helplessness and low self-worth can contribute to impulsive spending, financial mismanagement, or neglecting to plan for the future.

- o **Emotional Spending:** Many people use spending as a way to cope with negative emotions. However, this behaviour can lead to debt, financial instability, and a greater sense of loss of control over one's life.
- o **Failure to Invest in Personal Development:** Investing in education, skills training, or career coaching can open doors to new opportunities. However, individuals with a victim mentality often avoid investing in themselves due to a lack of belief in their potential, further perpetuating financial stagnation.

## 3. Dependence on Others

A victim mentality often leads to financial dependence on others, whether it is family, partners, or government assistance. While support can be essential in times of need, long-term dependence can erode self-confidence and reduce the drive to achieve financial independence.

- o **Lack of Financial Autonomy:** Dependence on others creates a sense of financial helplessness, reinforcing the belief that you are incapable of taking care of yourself. This can lead to strained relationships and a diminished sense of personal accomplishment.

## The Social Cost of Staying Stuck

# Living with Victim Mentality

The social implications of victim mentality are far-reaching, impacting relationships, social networks, and overall social well-being. People with a victim mindset often find themselves isolated, misunderstood, and disconnected from supportive communities.

1.  **Strained Relationships**

Victim mentality places a significant strain on personal relationships, including friendships, family dynamics, and romantic partnerships. The constant blame, defensiveness, and neediness associated with victim mentality can create a toxic environment that pushes others away.

- o **Erosion of Trust and Intimacy:** When blame and resentment become central to how you relate to others, trust and intimacy are eroded. Over time, relationships become strained, with conflicts unresolved and emotional needs unmet.
- o **Emotional Dependency:** Victims often rely heavily on others for validation, support, and emotional fulfilment, creating unbalanced relationships. This dependency can lead to resentment on both sides, as the victim feels unsupported and the other person feels burdened by constant demands.

2.  **Isolation and Loneliness**

As relationships deteriorate, individuals with a victim mentality may find themselves increasingly isolated. The sense of being misunderstood or unfairly treated by others often leads to withdrawing from social activities and avoiding new connections.

- o **Self-Imposed Isolation:** Feeling like a perpetual victim can lead to self-imposed isolation, where individuals cut themselves off from friends and family out of a belief that they will be rejected or hurt.

      o  **Loss of Support Networks:** Over time, the loss of supportive relationships leaves individuals without a crucial safety net, further exacerbating feelings of loneliness and helplessness.

3. **Reputation Damage**

Repeatedly playing the victim can damage one's reputation, both personally and professionally. People who consistently blame others and refuse to take responsibility are often seen as unreliable, negative, and difficult to work with.

      o  **Impact on Career and Social Standing:** A reputation for being negative or unaccountable can hinder professional opportunities and damage social standing. This can result in lost friendships, missed career advancements, and a lack of support from colleagues and peers.

## Missed Opportunities and Unfulfilled Potential

Victim mentality significantly limits personal and professional potential. By remaining stuck in a mindset of blame and helplessness, individuals miss countless opportunities to grow, achieve, and create a fulfilling life.

1. **Unrealized Dreams and Goals**

People with a victim mindset often abandon their dreams and goals, believing that success is impossible due to circumstances beyond their control. This resignation leads to a lifetime of what-ifs and regrets.

      o  **Fear of Failure:** The fear of failure keeps many victims from pursuing their passions or taking risks that could lead to success. The result is a life spent on the sidelines, watching others achieve what feels out of reach.

o **Settling for Less:** When you believe you are powerless, you settle for less in all areas of life—career, relationships, and personal achievements. This settling leads to chronic dissatisfaction and a sense of having never lived up to your potential.

## 2. Reduced Creativity and Problem-Solving Ability

Victim mentality stifles creativity and problem-solving skills. Instead of seeing challenges as opportunities to innovate, those stuck in victimhood view obstacles as insurmountable.

o **Lack of Initiative:** A victim mentality often leads to a lack of initiative, as individuals feel incapable of effecting change. This lack of action prevents them from exploring new ideas, developing skills, or finding unique solutions to problems.

o **Failure to Adapt:** In a rapidly changing world, adaptability is key to success. However, a victim mindset keeps individuals rigid and resistant to change, leading to missed opportunities in both personal and professional arenas.

## The Impact on Physical Health and Well-Being

The emotional and psychological burden of victim mentality also takes a toll on physical health. Chronic stress, anxiety, and negative thinking patterns can lead to a range of physical health issues.

## 1. Chronic Health Problems

The stress and emotional turmoil of a victim mindset can manifest as physical ailments. Chronic stress weakens the immune system, increases inflammation, and exacerbates conditions such as hypertension, diabetes, and heart disease.

- o **Sleep Disturbances:** Anxiety and overthinking can disrupt sleep, leading to insomnia or poor sleep quality. This lack of rest further diminishes physical and mental resilience, making it harder to cope with life's challenges.
- o **Fatigue and Low Energy:** The emotional drain of living as a victim leaves little energy for self-care, exercise, or healthy eating. This low energy perpetuates a cycle of physical decline and poor mental health.

2. **Poor Coping Mechanisms**

Many people with a victim mindset turn to unhealthy coping mechanisms such as overeating, substance abuse, or self-harm. These behaviours provide temporary relief but ultimately worsen physical and emotional health.

- o **Addiction and Substance Abuse:** Substance abuse is often used to numb emotional pain, but it exacerbates the cycle of victimhood and self-destruction. Addiction can lead to financial ruin, health problems, and further isolation.
- o **Neglect of Self-Care:** A victim mindset often results in neglecting basic self-care. Exercise, nutrition, and regular medical check-ups are often overlooked, leading to a decline in overall health.

**Conclusion**

Staying stuck in a victim mentality comes with a heavy price. The emotional, financial, and social costs can be overwhelming, and the impact on physical health and overall well-being is profound. Remaining in a cycle of blame, helplessness, and avoidance not only robs individuals of their potential but also leads to a diminished quality of life filled with missed opportunities and unfulfilled dreams. Recognizing these costs is a crucial step toward breaking free from the victim mindset and embracing a more empowered, accountable, and fulfilling way of living.

Living with Victim Mentality

# Chapter 11:

# Shifting the Mindset from Victim to Victor

Transitioning from a victim mentality to a victor mentality is a transformative journey that requires dedication, self-reflection, and a willingness to change deeply ingrained beliefs. This shift does not happen overnight, but with conscious effort and the right tools, anyone can move from feeling powerless to embracing a mindset of empowerment and growth. In this chapter, we will explore the concept of moving from victimhood to victory, discuss the importance of adopting a growth mindset, and emphasize the critical role of taking responsibility and reclaiming personal power.

### Understanding the Shift from Victim to Victor

The shift from a victim mentality to a victor mentality involves a profound change in how we perceive ourselves, our circumstances, and the world around us. It is about recognizing that, while we may not have control over everything that happens to us, we do have control over how we respond, how we think, and what actions we take.

1. **The Victim Mentality vs. Victor Mentality**
   - o **Victim Mentality**: This mindset is characterized by feelings of helplessness, blame, and self-pity. People with a victim mentality often see themselves as perpetual sufferers of life's challenges, believing that external forces control their fate. They focus on obstacles,

unfairness, and past traumas, allowing these factors to define their present and future.

o **Victor Mentality**: In contrast, a victor mentality embraces resilience, empowerment, and a proactive approach to life. Victors see challenges as opportunities for growth rather than insurmountable barriers. They focus on solutions, take responsibility for their actions, and believe in their ability to influence their own outcomes. This mindset is rooted in self-belief, accountability, and an unwavering commitment to personal growth.

2. **Shifting Perspectives: From Fixed to Growth Mindset**

A critical component of moving from victim to victor is adopting a growth mindset, a concept popularized by psychologist Carol Dweck. A growth mindset is the belief that abilities, intelligence, and talents can be developed through hard work, dedication, and perseverance. In contrast, a fixed mindset believes that these traits are innate and unchangeable.

o **Growth Mindset**: People with a growth mindset embrace challenges, persist in the face of setbacks, and see effort as a path to mastery. They learn from criticism and find lessons in failure. This mindset is essential for anyone looking to overcome self-limiting beliefs and rise above a victim mentality.

o **Fixed Mindset**: Those with a fixed mindset avoid challenges, give up easily, and view effort as fruitless. They are often threatened by the success of others and feel defeated by criticism. This mindset keeps individuals stuck in the belief that they cannot change their circumstances or improve themselves.

By adopting a growth mindset, you can reframe obstacles as learning experiences rather than insurmountable problems. This shift allows you to see yourself as a work in progress, where every challenge is an opportunity to grow, learn, and improve.

**Taking Responsibility and Reclaiming Personal Power**

One of the most critical steps in shifting from victim to victor is taking responsibility for your life. This does not mean blaming yourself for everything that happens, but rather recognizing the power you have over your responses, decisions, and actions.

1.  **The Power of Personal Responsibility**

Taking responsibility means acknowledging your role in your own experiences and taking ownership of your actions. It is about understanding that while you may not be responsible for everything that happens to you, you are responsible for how you handle those situations.

- o **Accountability vs. Blame**: Accountability is about ownership and action, whereas blame focuses on fault and punishment. When you take accountability, you empower yourself to make changes, learn from mistakes, and move forward. Blame, on the other hand, keeps you stuck in a cycle of defensiveness and helplessness.
- o **Empowerment Through Choice**: Recognizing that you have choices in how you respond to life's challenges is empowering. Every decision you make, from how you react to adversity to how you pursue your goals, shapes your path. This sense of agency is at the heart of a victor mentality.

2.  **Overcoming Self-Limiting Beliefs**

Self-limiting beliefs are deeply ingrained thoughts that hold you back from reaching your full potential. These beliefs often stem from past experiences, failures, or messages received from others that have been internalized as truths. Common self-limiting beliefs include thoughts like "I'm not good enough," "I will never succeed," or "I'm just not the type of person who can do this."

- o **Identifying Self-Limiting Beliefs:** The first step in overcoming these beliefs is to identify them. Pay attention to the negative self-talk that arises when you face challenges. Write down these thoughts and examine their origins—are they based on facts, or are they assumptions and fears?

- o **Challenging and Reframing Beliefs:** Once you have identified self-limiting beliefs, challenge them. Ask yourself: "Is this belief helping me or holding me back?" Reframe these beliefs into positive affirmations that reflect a growth mindset. For example, change "I can't do this" to "I'm learning how to do this."

- o **Visualization and Affirmations:** Visualization techniques and positive affirmations can help reinforce a victor mentality. Visualize yourself succeeding, overcoming obstacles, and achieving your goals. Affirmations like "I am capable," "I am resilient," and "I have the power to change my circumstances" can help reprogram your mindset.

3. **Reclaiming Your Narrative**

People with a victim mentality often feel defined by their past traumas and negative experiences. Reclaiming your narrative means taking control of your story and defining your identity on your terms.

- o **Rewrite Your Story:** Instead of viewing yourself as a passive character in your life story, see yourself as the author. You have the power to rewrite your narrative, focusing on your strengths, achievements, and the lessons you've learned along the way. This shift in perspective transforms you from a victim of circumstance to a survivor and thriver.

o **Embrace Resilience**: Resilience is the ability to bounce back from adversity. Cultivating resilience involves recognizing that setbacks are temporary and do not define you. By focusing on your ability to recover, adapt, and grow, you reinforce the victor mindset.

## Adopting a Solution-Oriented Approach

A critical difference between victim and victor mindsets is how each approaches problems. Victims dwell on problems, seeing them as insurmountable, while victors seek solutions and take proactive steps to resolve challenges.

1. **Focusing on What You Can Control**

Victims often focus on what they cannot control, such as other people's actions or external circumstances. This focus leads to feelings of powerlessness and frustration. Victors, on the other hand, focus on what they can control—their actions, responses, and attitudes.

o **Identify Controllable Factors**: In any challenging situation, make a list of factors within your control. For example, you may not be able to control a coworker's behaviour, but you can control how you respond, how you communicate, and how you manage your emotions.

o **Action-Oriented Thinking**: Shift from passive thinking to action-oriented thinking. Instead of saying, "I wish things were different," ask yourself, "What can I do to make things different?" This approach fosters a sense of agency and motivates you to take meaningful steps                                        forward.

2. **Setting Goals and Taking Action**

Setting goals is a powerful way to shift from victim to victor. Goals provide direction, purpose, and motivation, helping you to focus on what you want to achieve rather than what you fear or resent.

- o **SMART Goals**: Set SMART (Specific, Measurable, Achievable, Relevant, Time-bound) goals to create a clear path forward. Break down larger goals into smaller, manageable steps to avoid feeling overwhelmed.
- o **Celebrate Progress**: Acknowledge and celebrate your progress, no matter how small. Each step forward reinforces the belief that you are capable and in control of your journey.

3. **Developing Problem-Solving Skills**

Victors approach problems with curiosity and determination. Developing strong problem-solving skills is essential for overcoming obstacles and maintaining a proactive mindset.

- o **Identify the Problem Clearly**: Clearly define the problem you are facing. Avoid vague or emotional descriptions and focus on specific aspects that need resolution.
- o **Brainstorm Solutions**: Generate multiple solutions without immediately dismissing any as impossible. Consider different perspectives and weigh the pros and cons of each approach.
- o **Take Decisive Action**: Choose a solution and take decisive action. Even if the first attempt doesn't work, view it as valuable feedback that guides you closer to the right answer.

**The Importance of Self-Compassion**

As you shift from victim to victor, it's essential to practice self-compassion. Overcoming deeply rooted mindsets takes time, and setbacks are a natural part of the process. Be kind to yourself, acknowledge your efforts, and remember that growth is a journey.

### 1. Forgive Yourself and Others

Forgiveness is a powerful tool in reclaiming your power. Holding onto grudges or regrets keeps you tied to the past and prevents you from moving forward. Forgive yourself for past mistakes and forgive others who may have hurt you, not for their sake, but to free yourself from the burden of resentment.

### 2. Practice Self-Care

Prioritize self-care as part of your journey to becoming a victor. Engage in activities that nurture your mind, body, and spirit, such as exercise, meditation, journaling, or spending time in nature. Taking care of yourself reinforces the message that you are worth the effort and investment.

### Conclusion

Shifting from a victim mentality to a victor mentality is a transformative process that requires a change in perspective, the adoption of a growth mindset, and a commitment to personal responsibility. By embracing a victor mindset, you reclaim your power, break free from self-limiting beliefs, and open the door to a life of greater fulfilment, resilience, and success. Remember, the journey from victim to victor is not about perfection—it's about progress, perseverance, and the courage to rewrite your story on your terms.

# Chapter 12:

# Recognizing and Reframing Negative Thoughts

Negative thoughts can be powerful, shaping our perceptions, emotions, and behaviours in ways that reinforce a victim mentality. Learning to recognize and reframe these thoughts is crucial for breaking free from self-defeating patterns and adopting a healthier, more constructive mindset. In this chapter, we will explore techniques for identifying negative thoughts, strategies for challenging and reframing them, and practical exercises that can be incorporated into daily life for effective thought management.

**The Power of Thoughts and Their Impact on Mindset**

Thoughts are the building blocks of our reality. They influence our emotions, behaviours, and ultimately, the quality of our lives. Negative thoughts can create a cycle of despair, hopelessness, and stagnation, while positive thoughts can foster resilience, motivation, and growth. The key to transforming your mindset lies in gaining control over your thought patterns.

1. **The Connection Between Thoughts and Emotions**

Our thoughts are directly linked to our emotions. Negative thoughts often lead to negative emotions, such as anxiety, sadness, or anger, which in turn affect how we respond to situations. For example, if you think, "I always fail at everything," you're likely to feel discouraged and anxious, making it hard to take positive action.

2. **Common Negative Thought Patterns**

Negative thinking patterns are often automatic and deeply ingrained, making them difficult to recognize. However, once identified, these patterns can be challenged and changed. Here are some common negative thought patterns:

- o **Catastrophizing:** This involves expecting the worst-case scenario in every situation. For example, thinking, "If I make a mistake, I'll get fired," exaggerates the potential consequences and fuels anxiety.
- o **Black-and-White Thinking:** Also known as all-or-nothing thinking, this pattern involves seeing things in extremes, such as "I'm either a success or a complete failure." This mindset leaves no room for the complexities and shades of grey in life.
- o **Self-Blame:** This occurs when you blame yourself for things outside of your control, such as thinking, "It's my fault that everything went wrong." Self-blame erodes self-esteem and fosters guilt.
- o **Filtering:** This pattern focuses only on the negative aspects of a situation while ignoring the positive. For example, after receiving feedback at work, you might fixate on one critical comment and disregard all the praise.
- o **Mind Reading:** This involves assuming you know what others are thinking, usually in a negative way, such as "They must think I'm incompetent." Mind reading often leads to unnecessary conflict and misunderstanding.

### Techniques for Identifying Negative Thoughts

Identifying negative thoughts is the first step toward change. By bringing awareness to these thoughts, you can begin to challenge and reframe them.

1. **Mindfulness and Self-Awareness**

Mindfulness involves paying attention to the present moment without judgment. It helps you become more aware of your thoughts as they arise. When you notice a negative thought, instead of getting lost in it, acknowledge it and observe it without immediately reacting.

- o **Mindful Observation:** Practice noticing your thoughts throughout the day. Whenever you catch yourself feeling upset or stressed, pause and ask yourself, "What thought just crossed my mind?" Write it down if possible. This exercise helps you become more aware of automatic negative thinking patterns.

- o **Thought Journaling:** Keep a journal to record your thoughts, especially when you're feeling overwhelmed. Write down the situation, your thoughts about it, and how those thoughts made you feel. Over time, you will start to see patterns emerge, making it easier to recognize recurring negative thoughts.

2. **The "Catch-It, Check-It, Change-It" Technique**

This simple three-step method helps you catch negative thoughts in real-time and change them into more constructive ones.

- o **Catch It:** Notice when a negative thought pops up. For instance, if you're thinking, "I'm going to fail this presentation," acknowledge that thought.

- o **Check It:** Evaluate the thought. Is it based on facts, or is it an assumption? Is it helpful or realistic? Ask yourself questions like, "What evidence do I have that this thought is true?" or "Am I jumping to conclusions?"

- o **Change It:** Reframe the thought into a more balanced or positive one. Instead of thinking, "I'm going to fail this presentation," change it to, "I've prepared well, and I'll do my best. Even if it doesn't go perfectly, I can learn from the                                            experience."

3.  **Cognitive Behavioural Techniques (CBT)**

CBT is a widely used approach that focuses on identifying and changing negative thought patterns. Here are some specific CBT techniques to help you challenge negative thoughts:

- o  **Thought Record Sheets:** Use a thought record sheet to track your negative thoughts, the evidence for and against them, and how you might reframe them. This structured approach helps you see the irrationality of many negative thoughts.
- o  **Socratic Questioning:** This involves questioning your thoughts in a logical manner. Ask yourself questions like, "Is there another way to look at this situation?" or "What would I tell a friend who had this thought?"

4.  **Recognizing Cognitive Distortions**

Cognitive distortions are irrational thought patterns that skew our perception of reality. Recognizing these distortions can help you challenge and reframe them. Some common distortions include:

- o  **Overgeneralization:** Making broad conclusions based on a single event, such as "I failed once, so I'll fail at everything."
- o  **Personalization:** Taking responsibility for things beyond your control, such as "My friend didn't call me back, so I must have upset them."
- o  **Should Statements:** Using "should" or "must" to set unrealistic standards for yourself or others, like "I should always be perfect."

**Reframing Negative Thoughts into Positive, Constructive Ones**

Once you've identified a negative thought, the next step is to reframe it. Reframing involves changing your perspective to see the situation in a more positive or realistic light.

1. **From Catastrophizing to Problem-Solving**

If you're prone to catastrophizing, try shifting your focus from worst-case scenarios to potential solutions. Instead of thinking, "Everything will go wrong," ask yourself, "What steps can I take to make this situation better?"

   o **Example Reframe:** "I'm going to fail this exam" can be reframed as, "I'm feeling anxious about this exam, but I can study, ask for help, and do my best."

2. **From Black-and-White Thinking to Balanced Thinking**

Replace all-or-nothing statements with more balanced thoughts. Recognize that most situations have both positive and negative aspects.

   o **Example Reframe:** Instead of thinking, "I'm a complete failure," reframe it as, "I didn't succeed this time, but I'm learning and growing from the experience."

3. **From Self-Blame to Self-Compassion**

If you tend to blame yourself for things outside of your control, practice self-compassion. Acknowledge your efforts and recognize that everyone makes mistakes.

   o **Example Reframe:** Instead of thinking, "It's all my fault," reframe it as, "I did my best with the information I had at the time, and I can learn                    from                         this."

### 4.  From Filtering to Positive Reframing

Challenge your tendency to focus solely on the negatives by intentionally looking for positives in every situation.

> o  **Example Reframe:** Instead of thinking, "I messed up one part of the presentation," reframe it as, "Most of the presentation went well, and I handled the difficult part as best as I could."

## Practical Exercises for Daily Thought Management

Incorporating thought management exercises into your daily routine can help reinforce positive thinking and break the cycle of negativity.

### 1.  Daily Gratitude Practice

Cultivating gratitude can shift your focus from what's wrong to what's right in your life. Each day, write down three things for which you are grateful. This simple exercise trains your mind to look for positives, even in challenging times.

### 2.  Positive Affirmations

Positive affirmations are statements that reinforce a healthy self-image and encourage constructive thinking. Repeat affirmations like "I am capable," "I am resilient," and "I can handle whatever comes my way" to counteract negative self-talk.

### 3.  Visualization

Visualization involves mentally rehearsing positive outcomes. Spend a few minutes each day visualizing yourself successfully navigating challenges, achieving your goals, and handling stress with confidence. Visualization helps create a mental blueprint for success and reinforces a positive mindset.

### 4. Thought Stopping Techniques

When you catch yourself spiralling into negative thoughts, use a thought-stopping technique. This can be as simple as saying "Stop!" to yourself or snapping a rubber band on your wrist to interrupt the negative thought pattern. Then, immediately replace the negative thought with a more positive one.

### 5. The 5-4-3-2-1 Grounding Exercise

This grounding technique helps you refocus your mind on the present moment, breaking the cycle of negative thinking. Identify:

- o   5 things you can see,
- o   4 things you can touch,
- o   3 things you can hear,
- o   2 things you can smell, and
- o   1 thing you can taste.

This exercise helps centre your thoughts and shifts your focus away from negative patterns.

### 6. Journaling for Reflection and Growth

Use journaling as a tool to reflect on your thought patterns, track your progress, and set intentions for change. Write about situations that triggered negative thoughts, how you reframed them, and what you learned from the experience. Journaling can provide valuable insights and reinforce positive changes.

### Conclusion

Recognizing and reframing negative thoughts is a powerful way to take control of your mindset and break free from the victim mentality. By identifying harmful thinking patterns, challenging them with evidence, and consciously reframing your thoughts into more positive and constructive ones, you can create a more empowering mental landscape. Incorporating daily exercises to manage your thoughts will help reinforce these changes, leading to improved emotional well-being, better decision-making, and a more fulfilling life. Remember, the power to change your thoughts lies within you, and with practice, you can reshape your inner dialogue to support a mindset of resilience, growth, and positivity.

# Chapter 13:

# Building Resilience and Emotional Strength

Resilience and emotional strength are crucial elements in overcoming a victim mentality. Resilience refers to the ability to bounce back from adversity, setbacks, and challenges with a positive and proactive attitude. Emotional strength, on the other hand, is the capacity to manage and regulate your emotions effectively, allowing you to handle stress, disappointment, and uncertainty without succumbing to negative thought patterns. In this chapter, we will explore the importance of resilience in overcoming victim mentality, delve into techniques to build emotional strength, and discuss how these qualities can help you navigate life's challenges more effectively.

**The Importance of Resilience in Overcoming Victim Mentality**

Resilience is the foundation of a victor mentality. While a victim mentality keeps you trapped in feelings of helplessness and self-pity, resilience empowers you to take control of your life, learn from your experiences, and move forward with confidence. Building resilience shifts your focus from problems to solutions and from obstacles to opportunities.

1. **Resilience as a Key to Breaking the Cycle**

Resilience helps break the cycle of self-sabotage and negative thinking that often accompanies a victim mentality. Instead of seeing setbacks as confirmation of your perceived inadequacies, resilience allows you to view them as temporary challenges that can be overcome. This shift in perspective is essential for breaking free from self-defeating behaviours and adopting a more empowered approach to life.

## 2. The Role of Resilience in Personal Growth

Resilience is not about avoiding difficulties; it's about facing them head-on and growing from the experience. Every challenge you encounter offers an opportunity for personal growth, learning, and self-improvement. Resilient individuals embrace these opportunities, understanding that failure is not a permanent state but a stepping stone to success. By building resilience, you cultivate a mindset that sees adversity as a chance to develop new skills, gain insights, and build character.

## 3. How Resilience Enhances Problem-Solving and Decision-Making

Resilience enhances your ability to think clearly and make effective decisions, even in stressful situations. When you are resilient, you are less likely to be overwhelmed by negative emotions or paralyzed by fear. Instead, you approach problems with a solution-oriented mindset, exploring different options, weighing the pros and cons, and taking decisive action. This proactive approach enables you to navigate challenges more effectively and maintain momentum toward your goals.

### Techniques to Build Emotional Strength

Building emotional strength involves developing skills and strategies to manage your emotions, cope with stress, and maintain a positive outlook. Here are key techniques that can help you strengthen your emotional resilience:

## 1. Mindfulness: Cultivating Present-Moment Awareness

Mindfulness is the practice of paying attention to the present moment with an open and non-judgmental attitude. It helps you become more aware of your thoughts, emotions, and bodily sensations, allowing you to respond to situations with greater clarity and composure.

- o **Benefits of Mindfulness:** Mindfulness reduces stress, anxiety, and negative thinking by helping you stay grounded in the present rather than dwelling on past regrets or future worries. It enhances your ability to observe your thoughts without getting caught up in them, making it easier to challenge and reframe negative thought patterns.
- o **Mindful Breathing Exercise:** One simple way to practice mindfulness is through mindful breathing. Take a few minutes each day to focus on your breath. Inhale deeply through your nose, hold for a few seconds, and then exhale slowly through your mouth. Pay attention to the sensation of your breath as it enters and leaves your body. This exercise helps calm your mind and bring you back to the present moment.
- o **Body Scan Meditation:** Another effective mindfulness technique is the body scan meditation. Lie down comfortably and mentally scan your body from head to toe, noticing any areas of tension or discomfort. As you focus on each part of your body, breathe into that area and release any tension. This exercise promotes relaxation and helps you connect with your physical and emotional state.

2. **Self-Compassion: Treating Yourself with Kindness**

Self-compassion involves treating yourself with the same kindness, understanding, and support that you would offer a friend in distress. It is a powerful antidote to self-criticism and self-blame, which are common features of victim mentality.

- o **The Three Elements of Self-Compassion:**
  - **Self-Kindness:** Be gentle with yourself when you make mistakes or face difficulties. Instead of harsh self-judgment, offer yourself words of encouragement and understanding.
  - **Common Humanity:** Recognize that everyone experiences setbacks, failures, and challenges. You are not alone in your struggles, and it's okay to be imperfect.
  - **Mindfulness:** Be mindful of your emotions without exaggerating or suppressing them. Acknowledge your pain without letting it define you.
- o **Self-Compassion Exercise:** When you catch yourself engaging in negative self-talk, pause and reframe your thoughts as if you were speaking to a friend. For example, if you're thinking, "I'm such a failure," replace it with, "I'm having a tough time right now, but I'm doing the best I can, and that's enough." Practicing self-compassion helps you build resilience by fostering a supportive inner dialogue.

3. **Emotional Regulation: Managing Your Emotional Responses**

Emotional regulation is the ability to manage your emotional responses in a healthy and constructive way. It involves recognizing your emotions, understanding their triggers, and choosing how to respond rather than reacting impulsively.

- o **Identifying Emotional Triggers:** Keep a journal to track your emotional reactions throughout the day. Note the situations that trigger strong emotions and the thoughts associated with them. This practice helps you identify patterns and gain insight into the root causes of your emotional responses.

- o **The STOP Technique:** Use the STOP technique to regulate your emotions in the heat of the moment:
  - **S**top: Pause before reacting.
  - **T**ake a breath: Take a deep breath to calm your nervous system.
  - **O**bserve: Notice what you're feeling, thinking, and how your body is reacting.
  - **P**roceed: Choose a response that aligns with your values and goals, rather than reacting impulsively.
- o **Reappraisal:** Reappraisal is a cognitive strategy that involves changing the way you interpret a situation. For example, if you receive critical feedback at work, instead of viewing it as a personal attack, reframe it as an opportunity to learn and improve. Reappraisal helps reduce the intensity of negative emotions and fosters a more balanced perspective.

4. **Building a Support Network: The Power of Connection**

Social support is a critical component of resilience. Surrounding yourself with positive, supportive people can provide encouragement, perspective, and practical assistance during challenging times.

- o **Seek Out Positive Influences:** Identify people in your life who uplift and inspire you and make an effort to spend more time with them. These individuals can provide valuable feedback, help you stay accountable, and remind you of your strengths when you're feeling discouraged.
- o **Set Boundaries with Negative Influences:** Conversely, limit your exposure to individuals who drain your energy, criticize you, or

reinforce your victim mentality. Setting boundaries protects your emotional well-being and helps you maintain a positive mindset.

○ **Join Support Groups or Communities:** Consider joining groups or communities that focus on personal development, resilience building, or emotional support. Connecting with others who are on a similar journey can provide motivation, guidance, and a sense of belonging.

## How Resilience Helps You Bounce Back from Setbacks and Challenges

Building resilience and emotional strength equips you with the tools to bounce back from life's inevitable setbacks and challenges. Here's how resilience can transform your approach to adversity:

### 1. Embracing Challenges as Opportunities for Growth

Resilient individuals view challenges not as insurmountable obstacles but as opportunities to learn and grow. They understand that failure is a natural part of the learning process and use it as a stepping stone to future success. By embracing challenges with a growth mindset, you become more adaptable, resourceful, and willing to take risks.

### 2. Developing a Solution-Oriented Mindset

Resilience fosters a solution-oriented mindset that focuses on finding ways to overcome obstacles rather than dwelling on problems. When faced with a setback, resilient people ask, "What can I do to improve this situation?" rather than "Why is this happening to me?" This proactive approach empowers you to take control of your circumstances and move forward with confidence.

### 3. Maintaining Optimism and Hope

Resilient individuals maintain a sense of optimism and hope, even in difficult times. They believe in their ability to overcome challenges and see setbacks as temporary rather than permanent. This positive outlook helps them stay motivated, persevere through adversity, and remain open to new possibilities.

### 4. Learning from Setbacks and Adapting to Change

Resilience involves learning from setbacks and using those lessons to adapt and improve. Instead of repeating the same mistakes, resilient people reflect on what went wrong, identify what they can do differently, and make adjustments accordingly. This continuous cycle of learning and adaptation strengthens your problem-solving skills and enhances your ability to cope with future challenges.

### 5. Reducing the Impact of Stress on Your Health

Chronic stress can take a significant toll on your physical and mental health. However, resilient individuals are better equipped to manage stress because they have developed effective coping strategies. Techniques like mindfulness, emotional regulation, and self-compassion help reduce the negative impact of stress on your body and mind, leading to improved overall well-being.

### 6. Building Confidence Through Overcoming Adversity

Every time you overcome a challenge; you build confidence in your abilities. Resilience reinforces the belief that you are capable of handling whatever life throws your way. This growing sense of self-efficacy empowers you to take on new challenges with greater assurance and determination.

### Conclusion

Building resilience and emotional strength is essential for breaking free from the victim mentality and embracing a more empowered approach to life. By cultivating mindfulness, practicing self-compassion, regulating your emotions, and building a supportive network, you can develop the resilience needed to navigate life's ups and downs with grace and confidence. Resilience not only helps you bounce back from setbacks but also enhances your problem-solving abilities, fosters personal growth, and protects your overall well-being. Remember, resilience is not a fixed trait—it's a skill that can be developed and strengthened over time. With commitment and practice, you can build the emotional strength needed to overcome challenges, reclaim your personal power, and create a more fulfilling and resilient life.

# Chapter 14:

# Developing Self-Awareness

Self-awareness is the foundation of personal growth and the first step toward overcoming a victim mentality. It involves a deep understanding of your thoughts, emotions, behaviours, and how they influence your actions and decisions. By developing self-awareness, you can recognize the patterns that contribute to a victim mentality and take proactive steps to manage and change them. In this chapter, we will explore the role of self-awareness in recognizing and managing victim mentality, discuss ways to cultivate self-awareness through journaling, meditation, and reflection, and provide exercises to help you deepen your understanding of personal triggers and patterns.

## The Role of Self-Awareness in Recognizing and Managing Victim Mentality

Self-awareness allows you to see yourself objectively and identify the thought patterns, emotional responses, and behaviours that keep you stuck in a victim mentality. Without self-awareness, it's easy to fall into habitual ways of thinking and reacting that reinforce feelings of helplessness, self-pity, and blame. Here's how self-awareness plays a crucial role in breaking free from these limiting mindsets:

### 1. Identifying Negative Thought Patterns and Beliefs

Self-awareness helps you recognize the negative thoughts and beliefs that fuel a victim mentality. These might include thoughts like, "Nothing ever goes right for me," or "It's always someone else's fault." By becoming aware of these internal narratives, you can begin to challenge and change them, shifting from a mindset of helplessness to one of empowerment.

## 2. Understanding Emotional Triggers

Victim mentality is often driven by strong emotional responses, such as anger, frustration, or sadness. Self-awareness enables you to identify the specific situations, people, or events that trigger these emotions. Understanding your triggers helps you anticipate and manage your reactions more effectively, allowing you to respond thoughtfully rather than impulsively.

## 3. Recognizing Self-Sabotaging Behaviours

Self-awareness shines a light on self-sabotaging behaviours that keep you trapped in a cycle of victimhood. For example, you might procrastinate on important tasks because you fear failure or avoid difficult conversations because you feel powerless. By becoming aware of these behaviours, you can take steps to replace them with more constructive actions.

## 4. Taking Responsibility for Your Actions and Choices

Self-awareness fosters a sense of personal responsibility by helping you see how your actions and choices contribute to your current circumstances. It encourages you to move away from blaming others and start taking ownership of your life. This shift is essential for breaking free from victim mentality and reclaiming your personal power.

### How to Cultivate Self-Awareness

Cultivating self-awareness is a lifelong practice that involves introspection, mindfulness, and a willingness to confront uncomfortable truths about yourself. Here are some effective methods to develop self-awareness:

## 1. Journaling: Putting Your Thoughts on Paper

Journaling is a powerful tool for self-discovery and reflection. Writing down your thoughts, feelings, and experiences helps you process and understand them on a deeper level. It allows you to observe your internal world without judgment and gain insights into your thought patterns and emotional responses.

- o **Benefits of Journaling:** Journaling provides a safe space to explore your emotions, identify recurring themes, and track your progress over time. It can help you uncover hidden beliefs, clarify your goals, and develop a greater sense of self-awareness.
- o **Daily Reflection Journal:** Set aside 10-15 minutes each day to write about your experiences, thoughts, and feelings. Reflect on any challenges you faced, how you responded, and what you learned from the situation. Use prompts such as, "What triggered me today?" or "What negative thoughts did I notice?" This practice helps you identify patterns and develop a deeper understanding of yourself.
- o **Emotional Check-In:** At the end of each day, jot down a few sentences about how you felt and why. Note any emotional highs or lows and consider what might have contributed to these feelings. Over time, this can help you identify emotional triggers and recognize how your emotions influence your behaviour.

2. **Meditation: Cultivating Mindful Awareness**

Meditation is a practice that involves focusing your attention and quieting your mind to achieve a state of mental clarity and calm. It enhances self-awareness by helping you observe your thoughts and emotions without becoming attached to them. Through regular meditation, you can develop a greater understanding of your internal processes and learn to manage them more effectively.

- o **Benefits of Meditation:** Meditation reduces stress, improves concentration, and promotes emotional regulation. It helps you become more attuned to your inner world, allowing you to recognize when you're slipping into victim mentality and redirect your thoughts in a more positive direction.
- o **Mindfulness Meditation:** Find a quiet space where you won't be disturbed and sit comfortably. Close your eyes and take a few deep breaths to relax. Focus your attention on your breath, observing each inhale and exhale. If your mind starts to wander, gently bring your focus back to your breath. This practice trains you to be present and aware of your thoughts without judgment.
- o **Guided Meditation for Self-Awareness:** Use guided meditation apps or videos that focus on self-awareness and introspection. These meditations often include prompts to explore your thoughts, emotions, and physical sensations, helping you gain insights into your inner world.

3. **Reflection: Taking Time to Pause and Think**

Reflection is the practice of pausing to think deeply about your experiences, actions, and emotions. It involves asking yourself questions that encourage introspection and self-discovery. Regular reflection helps you identify areas for growth, recognize patterns of behaviour, and make more conscious decisions.

- o **Benefits of Reflection:** Reflection allows you to step back from your daily routines and consider how your actions align with your values and goals. It helps you gain perspective on your experiences, learn from mistakes, and celebrate your successes.
- o **Weekly Reflection Practice:** At the end of each week, set aside 30 minutes to reflect on the

past few days. Ask yourself questions such as, "What went well this week?" "What challenges did I face, and how did I handle them?" and "What can I do differently moving forward?" Write down your responses to track your growth and progress.

- ○ **Self-Reflection Questions:** Use prompts that encourage deeper introspection, such as:
  - ▪ "What are my core beliefs, and how do they influence my actions?"
  - ▪ "In what situations do I feel most vulnerable, and why?"
  - ▪ "What am I avoiding, and what fears are driving that avoidance?"

**Exercises to Deepen Understanding of Personal Triggers and Patterns**

To develop self-awareness, it's essential to go beyond surface-level observations and explore the deeper reasons behind your thoughts, emotions, and behaviours. Here are some exercises to help you uncover personal triggers and patterns:

1. **Trigger Tracking Exercise**

Triggers are external events or internal thoughts that evoke strong emotional responses. Identifying your triggers is a crucial step in managing your reactions and breaking free from victim mentality.

- ○ **How to Track Triggers:**
  - ▪ Keep a Trigger Journal: Whenever you feel a strong emotional reaction, take note of the situation, the emotions you experienced, and the thoughts that accompanied those emotions.
  - ▪ Identify Patterns: After a few weeks, review your entries to identify common triggers. Are there specific people,

situations, or thoughts that consistently elicit negative emotions?

- Reflect on Root Causes: Consider why these triggers affect you so strongly. Do they remind you of past experiences or touch on unresolved fears? Understanding the root causes can help you develop more effective coping strategies.

2. **Pattern Recognition Exercise**

Recognizing behavioural patterns is key to understanding how victim mentality manifests in your life. These patterns may include avoidance, procrastination, blaming others, or engaging in self-sabotage.

- o **How to Identify Patterns:**
    - List Common Behaviours: Write down any behaviours you engage in regularly that you suspect are related to victim mentality. For example, do you frequently avoid difficult tasks, make excuses, or dwell on past failures?
    - Analyse the Impact: For each behaviour, consider how it affects your life. Does it hold you back from achieving your goals, strain your relationships, or diminish your self-esteem?
    - Explore Underlying Beliefs: Ask yourself what beliefs drive these behaviours. Do you believe you're not capable of success, that others are out to get you, or that life is inherently unfair? Challenging these beliefs is essential for breaking the cycle.

3. **Self-Questioning Technique**

Self-questioning is a powerful tool for probing deeper into your thoughts and emotions. It involves asking yourself targeted questions to uncover hidden beliefs and motivations.

- o **How to Use Self-Questioning:**
    - Start with "Why": When you notice a strong reaction or unproductive behaviour, ask yourself, "Why did I react this way?" or "Why am I feeling this emotion?"
    - Go Deeper: For each answer, ask "Why?" again. Continue this process until you reach the core belief or fear that underlies your reaction. For example, if you felt angry during a meeting, you might discover that the anger stems from feeling disrespected, which in turn is tied to a deeper belief that you're not valued.
    - Reflect and Reframe: Once you've identified the core issue, consider how you can reframe it in a more empowering way. For instance, instead of believing, "I'm not valued," you might choose to believe, "I am responsible for asserting my value and communicating my needs clearly."

4. **Mirror Exercise**

The mirror exercise is a practice that involves looking at yourself in the mirror and engaging in an honest dialogue about your thoughts, emotions, and self-perceptions. It can be confronting but is highly effective in building self-awareness.

- o **How to Perform the Mirror Exercise:**
    - Find a quiet space where you can be alone with a mirror. Look into your eyes and start speaking aloud about how you're feeling, what you're

thinking, and any challenges you're facing.

- Pay attention to your immediate reactions. Do you feel uncomfortable, critical, or compassionate? Notice any judgments that arise.
- Use affirmations to counter negative thoughts and reinforce positive self-talk. For example, if you find yourself thinking, "I'm not good enough," counter it with, "I am learning and growing every day."

## Conclusion

Developing self-awareness is a transformative journey that empowers you to recognize and manage the thoughts, emotions, and behaviours that contribute to victim mentality. Through journaling, meditation, reflection, and targeted exercises, you can deepen your understanding of your personal triggers and patterns, allowing you to make conscious choices that align with your goals and values. Self-awareness not only helps you break free from self-defeating mindsets but also fosters personal growth, emotional resilience, and a more fulfilling life. By committing to the practice of self-awareness, you can reclaim your personal power and create a future defined by empowerment, responsibility, and self-compassion.

# Chapter 15:

# Setting Boundaries and Taking Control

Overcoming a victim mentality requires reclaiming your personal power, and one of the most effective ways to do this is by setting healthy boundaries. Boundaries are the limits and rules you set for yourself and others in order to protect your emotional, physical, and mental well-being. They help you take control of your environment and relationships, allowing you to prioritize your needs, maintain self-respect, and foster healthier interactions. This chapter will explore how setting boundaries can help you overcome victim mentality, provide practical steps to take control of your environment and relationships, and emphasize the importance of saying no, prioritizing self-care, and protecting your energy.

## How Setting Healthy Boundaries Can Help Overcome Victim Mentality

Boundaries are essential for overcoming victim mentality because they empower you to take responsibility for your own needs and protect yourself from being exploited or overwhelmed by others. Here's how setting boundaries can help you shift from feeling powerless to feeling in control:

1. **Establishing Self-Respect and Self-Worth**

Setting boundaries is an act of self-respect. It signals to yourself and others that your needs and feelings are valid and important. When you establish boundaries, you are affirming your self-worth, which is crucial in breaking the cycle of victim mentality. It shifts the focus from external validation and approval to internal self-validation.

## 2. Preventing Resentment and Overwhelm

People with a victim mentality often struggle to set boundaries, leading them to take on too much responsibility or become overextended in relationships. This can result in feelings of resentment, burnout, and helplessness. By setting clear boundaries, you can prevent overwhelm and protect your energy, creating a healthier balance in your personal and professional life.

## 3. Encouraging Personal Responsibility and Empowerment

Boundaries help you take control of your life by clarifying what you are willing and unwilling to accept from others. This promotes personal responsibility, as you are actively choosing how to engage with your environment and relationships. Instead of blaming others for your discomfort, you learn to advocate for your needs and take steps to protect your well-being.

## 4. Fostering Healthier Relationships

Boundaries are essential for maintaining healthy relationships. They create a clear understanding of each person's roles, expectations, and limits, reducing the likelihood of misunderstandings, conflicts, and co-dependency. Healthy boundaries also enable you to communicate more openly and honestly, strengthening trust and respect in your relationships.

## Practical Steps to Take Control of Your Environment and Relationships

Taking control of your environment and relationships involves setting and enforcing boundaries that support your well-being. Here are practical steps to help you establish boundaries and regain control:

1. **Identify Your Boundaries**

The first step in setting boundaries is to identify what your needs, limits, and non-negotiables are. This involves reflecting on your experiences, understanding what makes you feel uncomfortable or drained, and determining what you need to feel safe and respected.

- o **Assess Your Needs:** Think about different areas of your lifework, relationships, personal time—and consider what you need in each to feel balanced and content. For example, do you need more alone time, clearer communication, or respect for your personal space?
- o **Recognize Discomfort:** Pay attention to situations where you feel resentful, frustrated, or taken advantage of. These feelings are often indicators that a boundary is being crossed. Ask yourself, "What is happening here that makes me feel this way, and what boundary could help?"
- o **Define Your Limits:** Be clear about what behaviours you are willing to accept and which you are not. For instance, you might decide that you won't answer work emails outside of office hours or that you won't tolerate being spoken to disrespectfully.

2. **Communicate Boundaries Clearly and Assertively**

Once you've identified your boundaries, it's important to communicate them clearly and assertively. This can be challenging, especially if you are used to accommodating others or avoiding conflict, but clear communication is key to setting effective boundaries.

- o **Be Direct and Specific:** When expressing your boundary, be direct and specific about what you need. For example, instead of saying, "I need more respect," say, "I need you to speak to me calmly and avoid yelling during our discussions."

- o **Use "I" Statements:** Frame your requests in terms of your own needs rather than blaming or accusing others. For example, say, "I feel overwhelmed when I'm interrupted during my work time; I need quiet to focus," rather than "You always interrupt me."
- o **Stay Calm and Firm:** It's normal for people to push back when you set new boundaries, especially if they are used to you accommodating them. Remain calm, firm, and consistent in your communication, even if others react negatively. Reiterate your boundary calmly and do not feel compelled to justify it excessively.

3. **Set Consequences and Follow Through**

A boundary without consequences is merely a suggestion. It's essential to establish and communicate what will happen if your boundary is crossed, and then follow through consistently. This reinforces the seriousness of your boundaries and helps others understand that you are committed to protecting your needs.

- o **Define Consequences:** Consequences don't have to be punitive but should be clear and enforceable. For instance, if someone repeatedly interrupts you during work, the consequence might be that you won't respond to their messages until a designated break.
- o **Communicate Consequences:** Let others know what the consequence will be if they continue to violate your boundary. For example, "If you continue to speak to me disrespectfully, I will end the conversation."
- o **Enforce Consequences Consistently:** Consistency is key to maintaining your boundaries. If you set a consequence, follow through with it every time the boundary is

crossed. This reinforces that your boundaries are not negotiable and must be respected.

4. **Practice Saying No**

Saying no is a powerful boundary-setting tool that helps you protect your time, energy, and resources. Many people with a victim mentality struggle with saying no due to fear of rejection, guilt, or the desire to please others. However, learning to say no is essential for maintaining your boundaries and taking control of your life.

- o **Reframe "No" as Self-Care:** Instead of viewing no as a rejection or negative response, reframe it as a way to take care of yourself. Saying no means you are prioritizing your well-being and not overextending yourself.
- o **Start Small:** Practice saying no in low-stakes situations to build your confidence. For example, decline a minor request that you don't have time for or say no to an invitation that doesn't interest you.
- o **Use Polite and Firm Language:** You can say no without being rude. Phrases like "I'm unable to commit to this right now," "I have other priorities," or simply "No, thank you" are respectful yet assertive ways to decline requests.

**The Importance of Saying No, Prioritizing Self-Care, and Protecting Your Energy**

1. **Saying No as a Form of Empowerment**

Saying no is not just about rejecting demands—it's about asserting your right to choose how you spend your time and energy. When you say no to things that drain you, you create space for activities and relationships that nourish you. This helps you break free from the victim mentality, as you are actively making choices that prioritize your needs rather than passively accepting whatever comes your way.

## 2. Prioritizing Self-Care to Reclaim Your Power

Self-care is an essential aspect of boundary-setting and taking control of your life. It involves taking intentional actions to care for your physical, emotional, and mental well-being. Prioritizing self-care helps you maintain the energy and resilience needed to uphold your boundaries and make empowered choices.

- o **Physical Self-Care:** Engage in activities that support your physical health, such as regular exercise, healthy eating, and sufficient sleep. Physical self-care boosts your overall well-being and reduces stress, making it easier to manage challenging situations.
- o **Emotional Self-Care:** Practice emotional self-care by engaging in activities that soothe and uplift you, such as journaling, spending time with loved ones, or engaging in hobbies. Set aside time each day to connect with your emotions and nurture your inner world.
- o **Mental Self-Care:** Protect your mental energy by setting limits on activities that drain you, such as excessive social media use, negative news consumption, or toxic relationships. Focus on positive, growth-oriented content that inspires and empowers you.

## 3. Protecting Your Energy

Protecting your energy means being mindful of where and how you invest your time and emotional resources. This involves setting boundaries around who and what you allow into your life and being selective about the environments you engage in.

- o **Create a Supportive Environment:** Surround yourself with people who respect your boundaries, uplift you, and encourage your growth. Minimize contact with individuals who consistently drain your energy, violate your boundaries, or reinforce your victim mentality.

- o **Limit Exposure to Negative Influences:** Identify sources of negativity in your life—whether it's a toxic relationship, a stressful job, or harmful media consumption—and set boundaries to limit your exposure. This helps you preserve your mental and emotional well-being.
- o **Practice Energy Management:** Manage your energy by balancing work, social activities, and rest. Pay attention to how different activities affect your energy levels and adjust your schedule to ensure you have time to recharge.

## Conclusion

Setting boundaries and taking control of your environment and relationships are crucial steps in overcoming victim mentality. Boundaries help you reclaim your power, protect your well-being, and foster healthier, more balanced interactions with others. By learning to say no, prioritizing self-care, and protecting your energy, you can create a life that reflects your needs, values, and goals. As you practice setting and enforcing boundaries, you will develop a greater sense of control, empowerment, and self-respect, ultimately shifting from a mindset of victimhood to one of personal responsibility and resilience.

# Chapter 16:

# Cultivating a Positive Mindset

Shifting from a victim mentality to a more empowered and resilient mindset requires cultivating positivity. A positive mindset isn't about ignoring challenges or pretending everything is perfect; it's about choosing to focus on possibilities, finding solutions, and maintaining hope even in difficult situations. This chapter explores practical strategies to cultivate positivity, including the power of gratitude, affirmations, and visualization. We will also delve into how to build a daily routine that fosters positive thinking, reduces negativity, and highlights the importance of surrounding yourself with positive influences.

**Strategies to Cultivate Positivity**

Developing a positive mindset requires conscious effort and consistent practice. By integrating positivity into your daily life, you can reframe negative thoughts, build resilience, and foster a more hopeful outlook. Here are some effective strategies:

1. **Practicing Gratitude**

Gratitude is one of the most powerful tools for cultivating a positive mindset. It shifts your focus from what you lack to what you have, allowing you to see the good in your life, even when facing challenges. Regularly practicing gratitude can improve your mood, increase resilience, and foster a sense of contentment.

> o **Daily Gratitude Journaling:** Set aside a few minutes each day to write down three to five

things for which you are grateful. They can be as simple as a warm cup of coffee, a kind gesture from a friend, or the beauty of nature. This practice helps train your mind to notice the positives in your day-to-day life.

o **Express Gratitude to Others:** Take time to express your gratitude to the people in your life. This could be through a thank-you note, a heartfelt message, or a simple acknowledgment during a conversation. Not only does this strengthen your relationships, but it also reinforces a sense of appreciation and connection.

o **Gratitude Reflection:** When you're feeling overwhelmed by negative thoughts, pause and reflect on what you are grateful for in that moment. Shifting your focus to gratitude can help calm your mind and provide perspective, reminding you of the positives that exist alongside your challenges.

2. **Using Positive Affirmations**

Affirmations are positive statements that challenge negative thoughts and beliefs. By repeating affirmations, you can rewire your brain to think more positively and boost your self-esteem. This practice helps to counteract the inner critic that often fuels victim mentality and negative thinking.

o **Create Personalized Affirmations:** Develop affirmations that resonate with your personal challenges and goals. For example, if you struggle with self-doubt, use affirmations like, "I am capable and strong," or "I trust myself to make the right decisions." The key is to keep your affirmations positive, present-tense, and reflective of the mindset you want to cultivate.

o **Repeat Affirmations Daily:** Incorporate affirmations into your daily routine by saying them aloud in the morning, writing them down, or using them as reminders throughout the day. The more you engage with your affirmations, the more they will begin to influence your thinking and behaviour.

o **Visual Affirmations:** Place affirmations where you can see them frequently, such as on your bathroom mirror, computer screen, or phone background. Visual reminders keep your affirmations top of mind and reinforce the positive messages you're working to internalize.

3. **Visualization Techniques**

Visualization is a mental practice that involves imagining your desired outcomes as if they are already happening. This technique can help you build a positive mindset by focusing on your goals, enhancing motivation, and increasing your belief in your ability to achieve success.

o **Create a Vision Board:** A vision board is a collage of images, words, and quotes that represent your goals and aspirations. By creating a visual representation of what you want to achieve, you keep your focus on positive outcomes and reinforce your commitment to your goals.

o **Guided Visualizations:** Use guided visualizations or meditation apps to help you imagine achieving your goals or experiencing positive scenarios. For example, if you're preparing for a job interview, visualize yourself answering questions confidently and making a great impression. This practice can help reduce anxiety and boost your confidence.

o **Daily Visualization Practice:** Set aside a few minutes each day to close your eyes and vividly imagine your goals coming to fruition. Engage all your senses—see, hear, feel, and even smell what it's like to achieve your dreams. This immersive experience makes your goals feel more attainable and keeps you motivated to take action.

## Building a Daily Routine that Fosters Positive Thinking and Reduces Negativity

Cultivating a positive mindset is not just about isolated practices but about creating a daily routine that supports your mental and emotional well-being. By incorporating positivity into your everyday life, you build resilience against negativity and reinforce a more optimistic outlook.

### 1. Morning Routine to Set a Positive Tone

Your morning routine sets the tone for the rest of your day. Starting your day with positive habits can help you feel energized, focused, and ready to tackle challenges.

- **Morning Gratitude Practice:** Begin your day by acknowledging something you're grateful for. This simple act can set a positive mood and remind you of the good things in your life, creating a foundation of appreciation that carries you through the day.
- **Positive Intentions:** Set a positive intention for the day, such as "I will approach today with patience," or "I will seek out joy in my work." Setting intentions helps guide your mindset and actions, aligning them with the positive attitude you want to cultivate.
- **Affirmations and Visualization:** Incorporate affirmations and visualization into your morning routine. Take a few minutes to repeat your affirmations and visualize your day unfolding successfully. This practice primes your mind for positivity and keeps you focused on your goals.

### 2. Mindfulness and Meditation

Mindfulness and meditation are powerful tools for cultivating a positive mindset. They help you stay present, reduce stress, and build a more balanced perspective.

> o **Mindful Moments:** Incorporate mindful moments throughout your day where you pause, take a deep breath, and ground yourself in the present. These moments can help you break the cycle of negative thinking and bring your focus back to what matters.
>
> o **Meditation Practice:** Set aside time each day for meditation, even if it's just five to ten minutes. Guided meditations focused on positivity, gratitude, or self-compassion can help reframe your thoughts and promote a more positive                    outlook.

3. **Limiting Negative Influences**

Reducing exposure to negative influences is essential for maintaining a positive mindset. This involves being mindful of the media you consume, the people you surround yourself with, and the environments you engage in.

> o **Curate Your Media Consumption:** Be selective about the news, social media, and entertainment you consume. Limit exposure to content that triggers anxiety, anger, or despair, and seek out uplifting, inspiring, or educational material that fosters a positive perspective.
>
> o **Set Boundaries with Negative People:** While it's impossible to avoid all negative individuals, you can set boundaries to protect your energy. Limit your interactions with those who consistently drain you, and seek out supportive, positive connections that uplift you.
>
> o **Create a Positive Environment:** Surround yourself with reminders of positivity, such as inspirational quotes, calming artwork, or uplifting music. Creating an environment that

reflects your positive mindset reinforces your commitment to maintaining a hopeful and empowered outlook.

4. **Evening Reflection and Gratitude**

Ending your day on a positive note helps reinforce gratitude and positivity, setting the stage for a restful night and a fresh start the next day.

- o **Reflect on Your Day:** Spend a few minutes reflecting on the positives of your day. What went well? What did you achieve? Reflecting on your successes, no matter how small, helps you recognize your progress and reinforces a sense of accomplishment.
- o **Gratitude Practice:** Close your day with gratitude by writing down or mentally noting three things for which you are grateful. This practice helps shift your focus away from what went wrong and highlights the good, leaving you with a sense of peace and contentment.

## The Importance of Surrounding Yourself with Positive Influences

The people you surround yourself with significantly impact your mindset. Positive influences can inspire, motivate, and support you, while negative influences can drag you down and reinforce victim mentality.

1. **Choose Your Circle Wisely**

Be intentional about who you spend your time with. Seek out people who uplift you, encourage your growth, and share your values. Positive influences challenge you to see the best in yourself and inspire you to strive for your goals.

- o **Supportive Relationships:** Foster connections with people who are supportive, empathetic, and positive. These relationships provide a safe space for you to express yourself, gain perspective, and receive encouragement.
- o **Mentors and Role Models:** Look for mentors or role models who embody the positive mindset you aspire to cultivate. Their guidance, insights, and example can motivate you to overcome challenges and maintain a hopeful outlook.

2.  **Engage in Positive Communities**

Engage in communities or groups that promote positivity, growth, and well-being. Whether it's a hobby group, a fitness class, or an online community, connecting with like-minded individuals can provide a sense of belonging and reinforcement of positive values.

- o **Join Positive Groups:** Seek out groups that focus on personal development, health, creativity, or any area that interests you and aligns with your positive mindset goals. Being part of a positive community can help you stay motivated and inspired.
- o **Limit Toxic Interactions:** Recognize and minimize interactions with groups or individuals that perpetuate negativity, gossip, or criticism. Protect your mental space by engaging with people who reflect the positive, constructive mindset you wish to maintain.

**Conclusion**

Cultivating a positive mindset is a transformative journey that involves intentional practices, daily routines, and mindful choices about the influences you allow into your life. By embracing gratitude, affirmations, and visualization, you can shift your focus toward the positives and build resilience against negativity.

Creating a routine that supports your mental and emotional well-being, setting boundaries with negative influences, and surrounding yourself with supportive people are all critical steps in maintaining a positive outlook. This chapter's strategies will help you foster a mindset that not only overcomes victim mentality but also empowers you to live a more fulfilled and joyful life.

# Chapter 17:

# Seeking Support and Professional Help

Recognizing the need for support and seeking professional help is a crucial step in managing and overcoming victim mentality. While self-help strategies, such as positive thinking and resilience-building, are vital, they may not always be enough on their own. Therapy, coaching, and support groups provide additional guidance, perspective, and tools to help you break free from negative patterns and foster a healthier mindset. This chapter will explore the role of professional support in managing victim mentality, how to recognize when help is needed, and tips for finding the right support to make the most of your journey toward personal growth.

### The Role of Therapy, Coaching, and Support Groups

Seeking professional help can be transformative for individuals struggling with victim mentality. Professionals like therapists, coaches, and support group facilitators are trained to help you identify and work through the underlying issues contributing to negative thinking patterns and self-defeating behaviours. They provide a safe, non-judgmental space where you can explore your thoughts and emotions, gain new insights, and develop strategies for positive change.

1. **Therapy: A Deep Dive into Your Mindset and Emotions**

Therapy is a powerful tool for exploring the roots of victim mentality and addressing the emotional and psychological aspects that fuel it. Therapists can help you identify patterns of thought and behaviour that keep you stuck, process past traumas, and develop healthier coping mechanisms.

- o **Cognitive Behavioural Therapy (CBT):** CBT is one of the most effective therapeutic approaches for managing victim mentality. It focuses on identifying and challenging negative thought patterns and replacing them with healthier, more constructive ones. CBT helps you understand how your thoughts affect your feelings and behaviours, empowering you to break free from self-sabotaging cycles.
- o **Trauma-Informed Therapy:** If your victim mentality is rooted in past trauma, trauma-informed therapy can be particularly beneficial. This type of therapy acknowledges the impact of past traumatic experiences on your current mindset and behaviours and focuses on healing those wounds. Therapists use techniques like Eye Movement Desensitization and Reprocessing (EMDR) or somatic experiencing to help you process and integrate traumatic memories, reducing their hold on your present life.
- o **Psychodynamic Therapy:** This form of therapy delves into the subconscious mind to explore unresolved conflicts, past relationships, and deep-seated beliefs that contribute to victim mentality. By gaining insight into these hidden aspects of your psyche, you can understand how past experiences influence your present mindset and work towards releasing them.
- o **Mindfulness-Based Therapy:** Mindfulness-based approaches, such as Mindfulness-Based Stress Reduction (MBSR) and Mindfulness-Based Cognitive Therapy (MBCT), combine traditional therapeutic techniques with

mindfulness practices. These therapies teach you to stay present, reduce rumination, and develop a more balanced perspective on your thoughts and emotions, helping you break free from negative mental patterns.

## 2. Coaching: Focused Guidance and Accountability

While therapy often focuses on healing and deep emotional work, coaching is action-oriented and goal-focused. Coaches help you set realistic goals, develop strategies to achieve them, and hold you accountable throughout the process. Coaching can be particularly beneficial if you're looking to overcome victim mentality in specific areas of your life, such as career, relationships, or personal development.

- o **Life Coaching:** Life coaches provide guidance and support to help you identify limiting beliefs, set personal goals, and create action plans for positive change. They help you focus on the present and future, encouraging you to take responsibility for your life and make empowered choices.
- o **Career Coaching:** If victim mentality is impacting your professional life, a career coach can help you identify the barriers holding you back, develop confidence in your skills, and set clear career goals. Career coaching can address issues like job dissatisfaction, fear of failure, and procrastination, helping you build a more fulfilling work life.
- o **Health and Wellness Coaching:** For those struggling with victim mentality that affects their physical well-being, health and wellness coaches can provide support in areas like stress management, self-care, and healthy lifestyle choices. These coaches help you create a balanced approach to your physical and mental health, promoting overall well-being.

3. **Support Groups: Connecting with Others on the Same Journey**

Support groups offer a communal approach to overcoming victim mentality. These groups provide a safe space to share your experiences, hear from others who face similar challenges, and gain new perspectives. Being part of a supportive community can help reduce feelings of isolation and foster a sense of belonging and understanding.

   o **Peer Support Groups:** Peer-led groups allow members to share their stories, offer mutual support, and learn from each other's experiences. These groups can be found locally or online, focusing on various issues, such as anxiety, low self-esteem, or general personal growth.
   o **Therapist-Led Groups:** Some support groups are led by trained therapists who guide the discussions and provide professional insights. These groups often focus on specific themes, such as overcoming negative thinking, managing relationships, or building self-esteem. They combine the benefits of group support with therapeutic guidance.
   o **Online Communities:** Online support groups and forums offer accessible support from the comfort of your home. These platforms provide opportunities to connect with others globally, share your journey, and receive encouragement and advice in a digital space.

**How to Recognize When Professional Help is Needed**

Knowing when to seek professional help can be challenging, especially if you've been accustomed to handling things on your own. However, there are clear signs that indicate it might be time to reach out for support:

1. **Persistent Negative Thoughts and Emotions**

If you find yourself stuck in a cycle of negative thoughts, self-blame, or overwhelming emotions that you can't seem to manage on your own, it's a strong indicator that professional help is needed. Persistent feelings of sadness, anxiety, or hopelessness can significantly impact your quality of life and may require therapeutic intervention.

## 2.  Inability to Move Forward

When you feel stuck in life, unable to make decisions, take action, or pursue your goals due to fear, doubt, or a sense of powerlessness, seeking help can provide the clarity and direction you need. Therapists and coaches can help you identify the barriers holding you back and develop strategies to move forward.

## 3.  Relationship Struggles

If victim mentality is causing repeated conflicts or breakdowns in your relationships, it may be time to seek guidance. A therapist can help you explore how your mindset affects your interactions with others and provide tools to improve communication, set boundaries, and build healthier connections.

## 4.  Physical Symptoms and Health Issues

Chronic stress, anxiety, and negative thinking can manifest as physical symptoms, such as fatigue, headaches, or sleep disturbances. If your mental state is affecting your physical health, professional support can help address the underlying emotional issues contributing to these symptoms.

## 5.  Feeling Overwhelmed or Burnt Out

Feeling consistently overwhelmed, burnt out, or unable to cope with daily responsibilities is a sign that you need additional support. Professional help can provide you with strategies to manage stress, build resilience, and restore balance to your life.

# Living with Victim Mentality

**Tips for Finding the Right Support and Making the Most of It**

Finding the right support is essential to making meaningful progress. Here are some tips to help you navigate the process:

1. **Identify Your Needs**

Start by identifying what type of support you need. Are you looking for deep emotional healing, practical guidance, or a supportive community? Understanding your needs will help you determine whether therapy, coaching, or a support group is the best fit for you.

2. **Research and Ask for Recommendations**

Research potential therapists, coaches, or support groups in your area or online. Look for professionals with experience in addressing victim mentality, negative thinking, or related issues. Asking for recommendations from trusted friends, family, or your primary care provider can also lead you to reliable resources.

3. **Check Credentials and Specializations**

Ensure that the professional you choose is properly credentialed and specializes in the areas you need help with. For therapists, check for licensure and any additional certifications in trauma, CBT, or mindfulness. For coaches, look for relevant training and experience in the specific area you want to work on.

4. **Schedule Consultations**

Many therapists and coaches offer initial consultations to discuss your needs, answer questions, and determine if they're a good fit for you. Use this opportunity to assess their approach, communication style, and whether you feel comfortable working with them.

### 5. Set Clear Goals

Once you begin working with a professional, set clear goals for what you want to achieve. Whether it's reducing negative thinking, improving relationships, or building self-confidence, having specific goals will guide your sessions and keep you focused on your progress.

### 6. Be Open and Honest

To get the most out of your sessions, be open and honest about your thoughts, feelings, and experiences. Your therapist or coach is there to support you without judgment. Transparency allows them to provide the most effective guidance and interventions.

### 7. Commit to the Process

Personal growth takes time, and change doesn't happen overnight. Commit to the process, attend sessions regularly, and engage in any recommended practices or exercises outside of your sessions. Consistency is key to making meaningful and lasting changes.

### 8. Evaluate Progress and Adjust as Needed

Regularly evaluate your progress and discuss it with your therapist or coach. If you feel stuck or if the approach isn't working, don't hesitate to voice your concerns. A good professional will adjust their approach to better meet your needs or suggest alternative strategies.

### Conclusion

Seeking support and professional help is a courageous and empowering step in overcoming victim mentality. Therapy, coaching, and support groups provide the guidance, tools, and accountability needed to break free from negative patterns and build a healthier mindset. Recognizing when to seek help, finding the right support, and committing to the process are essential elements of your journey toward personal growth and resilience. By embracing the assistance of professionals, you can reclaim control of your life, nurture your well-being, and move confidently toward a more empowered future.

# Chapter 18:

# Rebuilding Relationships

Victim mentality and negative thinking can deeply impact your relationships, leading to conflicts, misunderstandings, and emotional distance. The patterns of blame, defensiveness, and self-pity associated with a victim mindset often strain personal connections, whether with friends, family members, or romantic partners. However, with commitment and the right approach, it's possible to repair and rebuild these relationships. This chapter will explore how to mend damaged relationships, improve communication, rebuild trust, and establish healthier dynamics to foster emotional intimacy.

## Understanding the Impact of Victim Mentality on Relationships

Victim mentality affects relationships in numerous ways, often creating a cycle of blame, resentment, and emotional disconnection. Recognizing how your mindset has influenced your interactions is the first step toward rebuilding damaged connections.

1. **Patterns of Blame and Defensiveness**: In relationships, those with a victim mentality often deflect responsibility, blaming others for their problems. This behaviour can lead to defensiveness from the other party, creating a cycle of conflict that erodes trust and intimacy.

2. **Emotional Withdrawal and Self-Pity**: Individuals with a victim mindset may withdraw emotionally when feeling hurt or misunderstood, resorting to self-pity

rather than addressing issues directly. This withdrawal can leave loved ones feeling shut out and frustrated, ultimately damaging the bond.

3. **Poor Communication and Misunderstandings**: Victim mentality can result in poor communication, where feelings are either bottled up or expressed in passive-aggressive ways. Misunderstandings are common when individuals fail to express their needs clearly or misinterpret the intentions of others through a lens of negativity.

4. **Neediness and Dependency**: A victim mindset can foster unhealthy dependency on others for validation and support. This dependency can create a dynamic where the other person feels overwhelmed, responsible for the victim's emotions, or pressured to "fix" their problems, leading to resentment.

5. **Resentment and Lack of Accountability**: Over time, the lack of accountability associated with victim mentality can breed resentment in both parties. One person feels overwhelmed by the other's negativity, while the other feels unsupported or misunderstood. This resentment, if left unaddressed, can lead to relationship breakdowns.

Recognizing these patterns and understanding their impact is crucial to rebuilding relationships. The next step is to actively work on repairing the damage by improving communication, rebuilding trust, and establishing new, healthier dynamics.

## Techniques for Improving Communication

Effective communication is the foundation of any healthy relationship. When communication breaks down, misunderstandings and conflicts arise. Improving how you communicate can help mend damaged relationships and foster deeper connections.

1. **Practice Active Listening**

Active listening is more than just hearing the words someone is saying, it's about truly understanding their message, feelings, and perspective. This involves maintaining eye contact, nodding or providing verbal acknowledgments, and avoiding interruptions.

> o **Show Empathy**: Acknowledge the other person's feelings without immediately responding with your own viewpoint. Phrases like "I understand that this is difficult for you" or "I hear what you're saying" show that you are genuinely engaged in the conversation.

> o **Reflect and Clarify**: Reflect back what you've heard to confirm understanding. For example, "So you're feeling frustrated because you don't feel heard, is that right?" This technique shows you are listening and helps clear up any miscommunications.

2. **Use "I" Statements**

"I" statements help express your feelings and needs without sounding accusatory. Instead of saying, "You never listen to me," try reframing it as, "I feel unheard when I try to share my thoughts." This approach reduces defensiveness and opens up space for constructive dialogue.

> o **Express Your Needs Clearly**: Clearly articulate what you need from the other person in a calm and respectful manner. This can help prevent miscommunications and allows your partner or loved one to understand how they can support you better.

> o **Avoid Blame and Criticism**: Focus on your feelings and what you can do to improve the situation rather than blaming the other person.

Constructive communication fosters collaboration, not confrontation.

### 3. Be Honest and Transparent

Transparency is vital to rebuilding trust and intimacy in relationships. Be open about your feelings, intentions, and mistakes. If victim mentality has led you to hide behind excuses or mask your true emotions, it's essential to break this pattern.

- **Admit Mistakes**: Taking responsibility for your actions, even when it's uncomfortable, is crucial for healing. Apologize when necessary and express your commitment to change.

- **Share Your Vulnerabilities**: Vulnerability fosters intimacy. Share your struggles and fears honestly, allowing the other person to understand you better and feel more connected.

### 4. Stay Present and Mindful

Mindful communication involves being fully present during conversations without letting past grievances or future anxieties cloud your judgment. Focus on the here and now and try to approach discussions with a calm and open mind.

- **Avoid Bringing Up Old Issues**: Stick to the topic at hand without dredging up past conflicts. Bringing up old grievances only rekindles negative emotions and diverts attention from resolving current issues.

- **Take Breaks When Needed**: If a conversation becomes too heated, it's okay to take a break. Stepping away temporarily allows both parties to cool down and return to the discussion with a clearer mind.

### Rebuilding Trust and Emotional Intimacy

Trust and emotional intimacy are often the most significant casualties of a relationship affected by victim mentality. To rebuild these crucial elements, both parties need to engage in consistent, positive behaviours that foster safety, connection, and mutual respect.

1. **Consistency and Reliability**

Rebuilding trust requires consistent actions over time. Be reliable in your words and actions and follow through on your commitments. Trust is slowly rebuilt when your behaviour aligns with your promises.

- **Keep Your Word**: Whether it's showing up on time, fulfilling promises, or being emotionally available, consistency is key. Small, everyday actions reinforce your reliability and sincerity.

- **Be Patient**: Rebuilding trust doesn't happen overnight. Be patient with the process and understand that it may take time for the other person to feel secure again.

2. **Forgiveness and Letting Go of Resentment**

Holding onto past hurts and resentments keeps both parties trapped in a negative cycle. Practicing forgiveness, both for yourself and the other person, is essential for moving forward.

- **Forgive Yourself**: Let go of self-blame and guilt associated with your past behaviours. Recognize that you are taking steps to change and be kind to yourself during the process.

- **Forgive Others**: Forgiveness doesn't mean condoning harmful behaviour, but it does mean releasing the grip of resentment that weighs down your relationship. Openly discuss grievances, seek closure, and work towards mutual understanding.

### 3. Re-establish Emotional Intimacy

Emotional intimacy goes beyond physical closeness; it's about being emotionally open and connected. Rebuilding emotional intimacy involves small, meaningful interactions that create a sense of closeness and understanding.

- **Share Experiences**: Spend quality time together, engage in shared activities, and create new positive memories. This fosters connection and helps overwrite past negative experiences.

- **Express Appreciation**: Regularly express gratitude and appreciation for each other. Simple gestures like saying "thank you" or acknowledging the other person's efforts can significantly enhance emotional bonds.

## Setting New, Healthier Relationship Dynamics

Rebuilding a relationship isn't just about repairing what was broken; it's also about setting the stage for a healthier, more fulfilling dynamic moving forward. This involves creating boundaries, fostering mutual respect, and being intentional about how you interact with each other.

### 1. Set Clear Boundaries

Healthy boundaries protect your emotional well-being and respect your needs and limits. Boundaries are not about pushing others away; they're about creating a safe space for yourself and your relationships to thrive.

- **Communicate Your Boundaries**: Clearly communicate what behaviours are acceptable and what aren't. For example, setting boundaries around how you handle disagreements can prevent escalations and maintain respect.

o **Respect the Boundaries of Others**: Just as you set boundaries for yourself, respect those set by the other person. Understanding and honouring each other's limits fosters mutual respect.

2. **Foster Mutual Respect and Support**

A healthy relationship is built on a foundation of mutual respect, where both parties feel valued and supported. Practice respectful communication, listen to each other's perspectives, and provide encouragement.

o **Encourage Each Other's Growth**: Support each other's personal growth and goals. Celebrate successes, offer encouragement during setbacks, and avoid criticism that undermines confidence.

o **Respect Individuality**: Recognize and appreciate each other's unique qualities, even when they differ from your own. Valuing each other's individuality helps maintain a balanced, supportive relationship.

3. **Create Intentional Positive Interactions**

Purposefully create positive interactions that enhance your relationship. Focus on small gestures of kindness, humour, and affection to maintain a sense of connection and joy.

o **Express Love and Affection**: Regularly express your love and appreciation through words, touch, or acts of service. Small gestures can significantly impact how connected you feel.

o **Engage in Constructive Conflict Resolution**: Disagreements are natural, but how you handle them makes a difference. Approach conflicts with a problem-solving mindset rather than a win-lose mentality and strive to understand each other's viewpoints.

## Conclusion

Rebuilding relationships damaged by victim mentality and negative thinking requires effort, patience, and a commitment to change. By improving communication, rebuilding trust, and establishing new, healthier dynamics, you can mend broken connections and create more fulfilling relationships. These steps not only help repair past damage but also set the foundation for stronger, more resilient relationships moving forward. The journey may be challenging, but the rewards of deeper connection, understanding, and emotional intimacy are well worth the effort.

# Chapter 19:

# Transforming Your Work Life

Victim mentality and negative thinking can significantly impact your work life, limiting career growth, job satisfaction, and professional relationships. However, by shifting your mindset, embracing a proactive attitude, and taking accountability for your actions, you can transform your work experience. This chapter will explore strategies to adopt a growth mindset at work, set career goals, seek opportunities, and handle workplace challenges with resilience and accountability.

## Shifting Your Mindset at Work: Embracing a Proactive Attitude

Transforming your work life starts with a mindset shift from reactive to proactive. A proactive mindset involves taking initiative, seeking solutions, and actively engaging with your work rather than passively waiting for things to happen. Here's how you can begin this shift:

1. **Identify Negative Work Habits**

Recognizing the negative work habits associated with victim mentality is crucial for change. Common patterns include avoiding accountability, blaming colleagues or supervisors for setbacks, and feeling powerless in the face of challenges.

> o **Reflect on Past Behaviours**: Take time to reflect on how your mindset has influenced your actions at work. For example, have you avoided taking on new responsibilities because you feared failure? Have you blamed others when projects didn't go as planned?

Understanding these patterns is the first step toward change.

o **Acknowledge the Impact**: Recognize how these behaviours have impacted your career. Avoiding responsibility or engaging in negative thinking can lead to missed opportunities, damaged professional relationships, and a lack of progress in your career.

2. **Adopt a Growth Mindset**

A growth mindset is the belief that your abilities and intelligence can be developed through dedication and hard work. This perspective contrasts with a fixed mindset, where you believe your skills and talents are set in stone. Embracing a growth mindset at work allows you to view challenges as opportunities for learning and growth.

o **Embrace Challenges**: Instead of avoiding difficult tasks, view them as chances to develop new skills. Accepting challenges willingly helps you build resilience and gain valuable experience that can propel your career forward.

o **Learn from Criticism**: Constructive feedback is essential for professional growth. Rather than taking criticism personally, use it as an opportunity to improve. Reflect on the feedback and apply it to your work to continuously enhance your skills.

o **Celebrate Effort, Not Just Results**: Recognize that effort is a key component of success. Celebrate your perseverance and dedication, even when the outcome isn't perfect. This mindset fosters continuous improvement and a sense of pride in your work.

3. **Take Ownership and Accountability**

Taking ownership of your actions is a powerful way to transform your work life. When you hold yourself accountable, you become more engaged, motivated, and committed to achieving your goals.

- o **Own Your Mistakes**: Mistakes are a natural part of any career. Instead of deflecting blame, take responsibility and focus on finding solutions. Acknowledging your errors demonstrates integrity and shows your willingness to learn and grow.

- o **Be Proactive in Problem-Solving**: When faced with obstacles, focus on what you can do to address the issue. Instead of waiting for someone else to fix the problem, take the initiative to find a solution. Proactive problem-solving builds confidence and establishes you as a valuable team member.

- o **Set Clear Boundaries**: Taking accountability also means setting boundaries to ensure you're working in a way that's sustainable and healthy. Communicate your limits respectfully, and don't be afraid to say no to tasks that compromise your work quality or well-being.

## Setting Career Goals and Seeking Growth Opportunities

To transform your work life, it's essential to set clear career goals and actively seek opportunities for growth. By defining what you want to achieve, you can create a roadmap that guides your actions and decisions.

1. **Define Your Career Vision**

Having a clear vision of where you want to go in your career provides direction and motivation. Your career vision should reflect your passions, strengths, and long-term aspirations.

○ **Identify Your Core Values**: Reflect on your core values and how they align with your career goals. Do you value creativity, leadership, or making a difference in your community? Knowing your values helps ensure your career path is fulfilling and aligned with your personal principles.

○ **Set SMART Goals**: SMART goals are Specific, Measurable, Achievable, Relevant, and Time-bound. For example, instead of saying, "I want to advance in my career," specify a goal like, "I want to achieve a management position within two years by completing leadership training and gaining project management experience." SMART goals provide clarity and make your objectives actionable.

○ **Break Down Long-Term Goals**: Long-term goals can be overwhelming if you don't have a plan. Break them down into smaller, manageable steps. For instance, if your goal is to become a team leader, start by taking on smaller leadership roles in projects or volunteer for tasks that demonstrate your leadership skills.

2. **Seek Learning and Development Opportunities**

Continuous learning is essential for professional growth. By seeking opportunities to develop your skills, you can increase your value in the workplace and position yourself for advancement.

○ **Take Advantage of Training Programs**: Many companies offer training programs, workshops, or courses to help employees enhance their skills. Take advantage of these opportunities to stay up to date with industry trends and expand your expertise.

- ○ **Pursue Certifications and Further Education**: Additional certifications or advanced degrees can provide a competitive edge in your career. Identify any qualifications that would benefit your role and take steps to achieve them, whether it's an online course, attending conferences, or joining professional organizations.

- ○ **Seek Mentorship**: Mentorship can provide valuable guidance and support as you navigate your career path. Seek out mentors within your organization or industry who can offer insights, advice, and constructive feedback.

3. **Network and Build Professional Relationships**

Building strong professional relationships can open doors to new opportunities and enhance your career. Networking isn't just about meeting people; it's about forming genuine connections that can provide support, collaboration, and mentorship.

- ○ **Attend Industry Events**: Attend conferences, workshops, and networking events relevant to your field. These events provide opportunities to meet like-minded professionals, learn from experts, and stay updated on industry developments.

- ○ **Engage on Professional Platforms**: Utilize platforms like LinkedIn to connect with professionals in your field. Share your insights, participate in discussions, and showcase your expertise to build your professional presence.

- ○ **Foster Relationships Within Your Organization**: Don't overlook the value of networking within your own workplace. Building positive relationships with colleagues, supervisors, and other departments can lead to collaboration, support, and potential career advancements.

## Overcoming Workplace Challenges with Resilience and Accountability

Workplace challenges are inevitable, but how you respond to them can define your career. Resilience and accountability are key to overcoming obstacles and maintaining a positive and productive work environment.

### 1.  Build Resilience in the Face of Setbacks

Resilience is the ability to bounce back from adversity. In the workplace, resilience allows you to navigate challenges, adapt to change, and maintain a positive outlook, even in difficult situations.

- o  **Stay Adaptable**: The workplace is constantly evolving, and adaptability is crucial for success. Instead of resisting change, embrace it as an opportunity to learn and grow. Flexibility in your approach will help you handle uncertainty and new challenges.

- o  **Maintain a Solution-Oriented Mindset**: When facing setbacks, focus on finding solutions rather than dwelling on problems. A solution-oriented mindset helps you remain proactive, reduces stress, and enhances your problem-solving skills.

- o  **Practice Stress Management Techniques**: High levels of stress can impact your performance and job satisfaction. Incorporate stress management techniques such as mindfulness, deep breathing, or regular exercise to maintain your resilience and overall well-being.

### 2.  Embrace Accountability in Team Dynamics

Accountability is crucial in team environments, where collaboration and mutual support drive success. Taking responsibility for your role within a team fosters trust, improves communication, and leads to better outcomes.

- o **Communicate Transparently**: Open communication builds trust within a team. Be transparent about your progress, challenges, and needs. This honesty creates a supportive environment where team members can work together effectively.

- o **Support Your Colleagues**: Accountability also means supporting your colleagues in their roles. Offer help when needed, acknowledge their contributions, and provide constructive feedback. A positive team dynamic enhances everyone's performance and satisfaction.

- o **Own Your Role in Team Success**: Recognize that your contributions impact the entire team. Whether it's meeting deadlines, maintaining quality, or supporting team goals, take ownership of your responsibilities and strive to add value.

3.  **Handle Conflicts with Professionalism and Respect**

Workplace conflicts are common but handling them with professionalism and respect is essential for maintaining a healthy work environment. Avoiding conflict or approaching it defensively only perpetuates tension.

- o **Address Issues Directly**: Don't let conflicts fester. Address issues directly and respectfully, focusing on the behaviour or situation rather than personal attacks. This approach promotes understanding and resolution.

- o **Seek Compromise and Collaboration**: Be willing to compromise and find collaborative solutions. Approach conflicts with a mindset of working together to find the best outcome rather than trying to "win" the argument.

- o **Maintain Professionalism**: Even in challenging situations, maintain your professionalism. Keep your emotions in check, listen actively, and aim for a constructive dialogue that moves toward resolution.

## Conclusion

Transforming your work life requires a shift in mindset, proactive strategies, and a commitment to personal and professional growth. By embracing accountability, setting clear goals, and building resilience, you can overcome workplace challenges and create a more fulfilling and successful career. Whether it's through improving communication, seeking learning opportunities, or fostering strong professional relationships, the steps you take today will shape your work life for the better, leading to greater satisfaction, achievement, and personal empowerment.

# Chapter 20:

# Living a Life of Empowerment and Purpose

Reaching the end of the journey from victim mentality to an empowered and purposeful life is both a celebration and a new beginning. Living a life of empowerment and purpose involves creating a long-term plan that maintains a positive mindset, setting meaningful goals, and pursuing passions with intent and clarity. This chapter will explore how to sustain an empowered mindset, the significance of setting and pursuing meaningful goals, and how to fully embrace a life of purpose and fulfilment.

## Creating a Long-Term Plan for Maintaining a Positive and Empowered Mindset

To live a life of empowerment, it's crucial to develop a long-term plan that fosters a positive mindset and continuous personal growth. Maintaining this mindset involves regular self-reflection, goal setting, and adopting habits that reinforce empowerment.

1. **Regular Self-Reflection**

Self-reflection allows you to assess your progress, acknowledge achievements, and identify areas for improvement. It's a practice that helps you stay connected to your values, goals, and the purpose driving your actions.

> o **Keep a Journal**: Maintaining a journal is a powerful tool for self-reflection. Regularly write about your experiences, feelings, and thoughts. Reflect on what's working well and what could

be improved. Journaling helps you track your growth and stay aligned with your purpose.

o **Set Aside Reflection Time**: Designate time each week or month for self-reflection. Use this time to review your goals, evaluate your progress, and adjust your plans as needed. This practice ensures that you remain focused and proactive in your personal development.

o **Seek Feedback**: Engage with trusted mentors, friends, or coaches to gain external perspectives on your progress. Feedback can provide valuable insights and help you stay on track with your goals.

2. **Adopt Empowering Habits**

Developing habits that reinforce an empowered mindset is essential for long-term success. These habits include positive self-talk, continuous learning, and self-care practices that support your well-being.

o **Practice Positive Self-Talk**: Replace negative self-talk with affirmations and constructive inner dialogue. Regularly remind yourself of your strengths, achievements, and potential. Positive self-talk boosts confidence and reinforces an empowered mindset.

o **Commit to Lifelong Learning**: Embrace opportunities for growth and learning. Whether through formal education, reading, or skill development, staying curious and engaged helps you continuously evolve and adapt.

o **Prioritize Self-Care**: Taking care of your physical, emotional, and mental health is crucial for maintaining empowerment. Engage in activities that nourish your well-being, such as exercise, meditation, and hobbies that bring you joy.

3. **Set and Revisit Goals**

Setting meaningful goals provides direction and motivation. It's important to regularly revisit and adjust your goals to ensure they align with your evolving aspirations and purpose.

- o **Create a Vision Board**: Visualizing your goals through a vision board can be a powerful motivator. Include images, quotes, and symbols that represent your aspirations. Place the board in a visible location to remind yourself of your vision regularly.

- o **Break Goals into Actionable Steps**: Divide long-term goals into smaller, actionable steps. This approach makes your goals more manageable and helps you track progress. Celebrate each milestone to maintain motivation.

- o **Review and Adjust Goals**: Periodically review your goals and adjust them based on your progress and changing priorities. Flexibility in your goals allows you to adapt to new opportunities and challenges.

## Setting Meaningful Goals and Pursuing Passions

Setting meaningful goals and pursuing passions are integral to living a life of purpose and fulfilment. These elements provide direction, motivation, and a sense of satisfaction that comes from aligning your actions with your values and interests.

1. **Identify Your Passions and Values**

Understanding your passions and core values is crucial for setting goals that resonate with your true self. Reflect on what inspires and excites you, and how these passions align with your values.

- o **Explore Your Interests**: Take time to explore various activities, hobbies, and interests. Identify what brings you joy and fulfilment. Passion often emerges from activities that resonate deeply with your personal values and interests.

- o **Define Your Core Values**: Clarify the values that guide your decisions and actions. Values such as integrity, creativity, or helping others can serve as a foundation for setting meaningful goals and pursuing a fulfilling life.

- o **Align Goals with Values**: Ensure that your goals align with your core values. When your goals reflect what you value most, you're more likely to stay motivated and committed to achieving them.

2. **Set SMART Goals**

SMART goals—Specific, Measurable, Achievable, Relevant, and Time-bound—provide a clear framework for setting and achieving your aspirations. This approach ensures that your goals are actionable and realistic.

- o **Be Specific**: Clearly define what you want to achieve. For example, instead of saying "I want to improve my career," set a specific goal such as "I want to complete a certification in project management within six months."

- o **Measure Progress**: Establish criteria for measuring your progress. This could involve tracking milestones, deadlines, or quantifiable outcomes. Regularly review your progress to stay on track and make adjustments as needed.

- o **Ensure Achievability**: Set goals that are challenging yet achievable. Consider your current resources, skills, and constraints when setting goals. Stretching yourself is important but ensure that your goals are realistic.

- o **Keep Goals Relevant**: Align your goals with your broader life purpose and values. Ensure that your goals contribute to your overall vision and aspirations. Relevant goals are more motivating and fulfilling.

- o **Set Time-bound Deadlines**: Assign deadlines to your goals to create a sense of urgency and accountability. Deadlines help you stay focused and motivated, and they provide a timeline for achieving your objectives.

3. **Pursue Passions with Intent**

Pursuing passions requires intentionality and commitment. By integrating your passions into your daily life, you create a sense of purpose and fulfilment.

- o **Create a Passion Plan**: Develop a plan for incorporating your passions into your life. This could involve dedicating time to hobbies, seeking career opportunities that align with your interests, or pursuing creative projects.

- o **Take Action**: Actively pursue opportunities related to your passions. Whether it's starting a new venture, volunteering, or taking a class, taking action helps you make progress toward living a life aligned with your interests.

- o **Stay Open to New Experiences**: Be open to exploring new passions and interests. Life is dynamic, and your passions may evolve over time. Embrace new experiences as opportunities for growth and self-discovery.

## Celebrating the Journey from Victim to Victor

Embracing a life of purpose and fulfilment involves celebrating the journey you've undertaken from victim mentality to a position of empowerment and purpose. This celebration acknowledges your growth, resilience, and achievements, and it reinforces your commitment to living a fulfilling life.

### 1. Acknowledge Your Achievements

Recognize and celebrate the milestones and accomplishments you've achieved along the way. Reflect on how far you've come and the challenges you've overcome.

- **Celebrate Milestones**: Mark significant achievements and milestones in your journey. This could involve celebrating personal or professional accomplishments, such as reaching a career goal, completing a project, or overcoming a personal challenge.

- **Share Your Success**: Share your achievements with supportive friends, family, or colleagues. Celebrating with others fosters a sense of community and provides positive reinforcement.

### 2. Reflect on Growth and Transformation

Take time to reflect on your growth and transformation. Acknowledge the changes you've made in your mindset, behaviours, and life direction.

- **Document Your Journey**: Consider documenting your journey through writing, photos, or other creative means. This record serves as a reminder of your progress and a source of inspiration for future endeavours.

o **Reflect on Lessons Learned**: Reflect on the lessons you've learned throughout your journey. Consider how these lessons have shaped your perspective and contributed to your personal development.

3. **Embrace a Future of Purpose and Fulfilment**

Embracing a life of purpose and fulfilment involves looking forward with optimism and intention. Set new goals, pursue new passions, and continue to cultivate a positive mindset as you move forward.

o **Set New Aspirations**: As you achieve your current goals, set new aspirations to continue growing and evolving. Embrace new challenges and opportunities that align with your vision and purpose.

o **Maintain a Growth Mindset**: Continue to foster a growth mindset as you navigate new experiences. Stay curious, open-minded, and proactive in your pursuit of personal and professional development.

o **Live with Intention**: Make intentional choices that align with your values and goals. Approach each day with purpose and prioritize activities and relationships that contribute to your sense of fulfilment.

**Conclusion**

Living a life of empowerment and purpose is a continuous journey that involves maintaining a positive mindset, setting meaningful goals, and pursuing your passions with intention. By creating a long-term plan that fosters empowerment, embracing growth, and celebrating your achievements, you build a foundation for a fulfilling and purposeful life. As you transition from a victim mentality to a position of empowerment, remember that this journey is not just about overcoming challenges but about embracing a future filled with possibilities, growth, and fulfilment. Celebrate your progress, stay committed to your purpose, and continue to live with intention and joy.

# Acknowledgments

Dear Readers,

Thank you for joining me on this transformative journey through the pages of this book. Your commitment to exploring and understanding victim mentality, negative thinking, and the path to empowerment and purpose is truly commendable. I am deeply grateful for the opportunity to share this exploration with you.

Writing this book has been a profoundly personal and enriching experience. It is my sincere hope that the insights and strategies presented here have provided you with valuable tools and perspectives to foster positive change in your life. The journey from victim mentality to living a life of empowerment and purpose is both challenging and rewarding, and I am honoured to have been a part of your journey.

Every chapter of this book has been crafted with care, drawing from a blend of research, personal experience, and professional insights. My aim has been to offer not just theoretical knowledge, but practical, actionable steps to help you overcome the limitations imposed by negative thinking and embrace a more fulfilling, empowered existence.

Your willingness to reflect, learn, and grow demonstrates a remarkable dedication to personal development. It is my hope that the principles and techniques discussed here will continue to guide and support you as you navigate your path forward. Remember, each step you take toward understanding and overcoming these challenges is a step toward a more empowered and purposeful life.

I encourage you to continue applying the strategies outlined in this book, to seek support when needed, and to celebrate your progress along the way. The journey toward empowerment is ongoing, and each day presents new opportunities for growth and self-discovery.

Once again, thank you for reading and for investing in yourself through this book. Your journey from victim to victor is one of strength, resilience, and personal triumph. I am deeply honoured to have been a part of that journey and wish you continued success and fulfilment as you embrace a life of purpose and empowerment.

With sincere gratitude,


Courtney

Courtney Collins

Living with Victim Mentality

Living with Victim Mentality

Made in United States
North Haven, CT
16 March 2025

66874245R00095